STELLA PETROU CONCHA

The Mastery Journal

The Intelligence of Self Mastery

Copyright © 2021 Stella Petrou Concha

All rights reserved, except as permitted under the *Australian Copyright Act 1968*. No part of this publication may be reproduced, distributed, or transmitted in any form or by any means, including photocopying, recording, or other electronic or mechanical methods, without the prior written permission of the publisher, except in the case of brief quotations embodied in critical reviews and certain other noncommercial uses permitted by copyright law.

Every effort has been made to trace and seek permission for the use of the original source material used within this book. Where the attempt has been unsuccessful, the publisher would be pleased to hear from the author/publisher to rectify any omission.

First published in 2021 by Hambone Publishing
Melbourne, Australia

Editing by Mish Phillips and Catherine Kane
Design by Adair Imrie

For information about this title, contact:
Stella Petrou Concha
www.stellapetrouconcha.com.au

ISBN 978-1-922357-28-1 (paperback)
ISBN 978-1-922357-29-8 (hardback)

This Journal Belongs To...

....

To my father;
for teaching me the magic of affirmations
and the power of the mind.

Contents

How it Works 11

Morning Ritual 12

    One thing I can get excited about today is...

    I am grateful this morning because ...

    The word that best describes the person I want to be today is...

    One bold action I can take today is...

    'Coach Me' to myself: Today you need to remember that...

    I would know today is a good day by...

Evening Ritual 14

    Tonight I am grateful because...

    A situation I handled well today was...

    Something I learnt today was...

    I could have made today even better if...

    One thing I will let go of for tomorrow is...

    One thing I will commit to tomorrow is...

Focus Daily Planner 16

Affirmation 16

Connect and Communicate 16

    Who must I connect with today?

    Who must I communicate with today?

Tasks and Actions 17

    What tasks must be completed today?

    What actions do I need to take today to execute on my vision or work strategy?

About The Half Reflection 17

Exercise: The Half Reflection 282

About Stone Heart, Light Heart 284

About the Author 287

Your word is your wand.
What you say repeatedly becomes your reality.

How It Works

The Mastery Journal has been created as a companion to **Stone Heart, Light Heart: The Intelligence of Self Mastery.**

The journey of self mastery is a commitment to a way of life. Prioritising your self and the ownership of your personal space takes discipline and a deep respect for the process of understanding yourself and the structures that make up your behaviours. Putting in daily habits to support your self mastery journey can be as simple as a daily meditation, a set period to exercise, or a commitment to daily reflection and intention setting.

A mantra that I introduce in **Stone Heart, Light Heart** is...

> *"Your inner world is reflected in your outer world. If you want to make a change in your outer world, change your inner world".*

The Mastery Journal commands your attention to your inner world. It enables you to implement powerful daily habits using meaningful self reflection questions which will set your outer world up for mastery.

Morning Ritual

One thing I can get excited today about is...

The mind can be easily distracted by the things that aren't working for us, so we must work extra hard to get it focused on the activities that are going well. This prompt gets you to acknowledge the activities in your day that bring you joy and excitement. These joys may be as simple as a scheduled coffee with a loved one, a day with no meetings or a special event you are anticipating. Giving your unconscious mind the opportunity to acknowledge that which excites you helps build high-vibrational energy and positive momentum around your day.

I am grateful this morning because...

This is a simple prompt that allows us to focus on the abundance of opportunities we are given each day to be grateful for. A state of gratitude has been shown to elevate our vibrational energy, improving mood, sleep and reducing stress. In reflecting on this prompt, challenge yourself to take your gratitude beyond loved ones, family and friends. Identify gratitude in all areas of life.

The word that best describes the person I want to be today is...

This prompt is designed for you to connect with your higher self, giving you access to information regarding the attributes that devise your best self. Your best self may need to change day to day depending on what you perceive the current challenges to be. This prompt asks you to describe the behaviours of your best self through the lens of the day at hand. Examples include "calm, fearless, bold, detached, or accepting".

One bold action I can take today is...

Focus here on the action that is most bold or significant and will have a ripple effect on many other tasks or moments in your day. This might be ringing your mum to tell her you love her, or connecting with a work colleague to provide some positive feedback on a recent presentation they delivered. This activity unlocks the intelligence in your unconscious mind, which often knows the solutions to your great challenges and questions. Take this time to be silent and let your unconscious reveal to you the areas craving focus in your own unique navigating system. This is an important habit of self mastery.

'Coach Me' to myself: Today you need to remember that...

Your higher conscious mind has great intelligence that often is clouded by the judgements of the ego. Formally calling this part of your mind 'Coach' allows you to tap into this intelligence. It's a way of asking the higher conscious mind for intelligence to guide you today into alignment with your best self. If your higher conscious mind was a wise sage, what advice would it give you today?

I would know today is a good day if...

This prompt helps you to prioritise and home in on one thing that that would make today a good day. Just that one thing. It could be exercising, playing with the kids or nailing that work presentation. This will change day to day depending on what's more important or burning at the time. Delivering on your most important task enables you to extract meaning from your day and acknowledge that the day was a good one. This then propels positive momentum. Remember that Rome wasn't built in a day. Taking small positive steps towards your goals is the key to life-long self mastery.

Evening Ritual

Tonight I am grateful because...

This is an invitation to reflect on your day and identify what you are grateful for. This helps you to realign yourself with high-vibrational thoughts before you rest for sleep.

A situation I handled well today was...

This prompt helps you to acknowledge the situations you handled well. It's easy for the conscious mind and ego to identify gaps or issues, and drag us into negative thought loops of not being 'enough'. This prompt breaks that and helps you build a positive relationship with yourself. It's the start of self love.

Something I learnt today was...

Part of self mastery is failing and failing forward. Much of life's learning comes from challenges and failures. Here is a space to reflect on what you have learnt from the day. It may be an idea that has been reinforced for you or a hard learning coming from failure. There are gifts of intelligence in every moment. Allow yourself the time to reflect and identify them.

I could have made today even better by...

This question is a lens through which we may seek micro improvements. Looking for 1% improvements over time adds up, enabling you to create the life you envision.

One thing I will let go of for tomorrow is...

This prompt asks you to reflect and identify a habit, thought or behaviour from your day that no longer serves you. In identifying this, you have the opportunity to make a commitment to let go of it. In this way, you prevent your past unwanted habits or thoughts from carrying forward into your future. If you don't take the time to reflect on your thoughts and habits, then your past will ultimately become your predictable future. It's important we take the time for this one.

One thing I will commit to tomorrow is...

This prompt allows you to make a new commitment to yourself on a daily basis. Every day is a new day. Every moment is a new moment. We must remind ourselves that we have the opportunity in every moment to create the life we want. It all starts with your daily commitment.

Focus Daily Planner

This daily focused planner is a series of questions that gets you focused on action and execution. It considers people you need to communicate with and activities that help you move closer to achieving your strategic work objectives or vision.

Affirmation

Reflecting on your morning ritual, what is the affirmation you need to say to yourself today to keep you wholly aligned and on track? Here are some examples:

> "Slow is smooth, smooth is fast, be slow in all my activities, I take my time and do everything with delicacy."

> "I am the curator of my life, that which I say becomes my reality."

Connect and Communicate

Who must I connect with today?

There will be people whom you need to connect with, business or personal. These connections will enable you to fulfill the tasks or goals for your day.

Who must I communicate with today?

This question asks you to consider the people you need to actively communicate with. What is the message? What is the outcome you are looking for from this communication? This activity will again help you achieve the outcomes of your day. Communication is the axis that allows your world to spin smoothly. Have a think about what your messages are and who needs to receive them.

Tasks and Actions

What tasks must be completed today?

This is as simple as your to-do list for the day. Often your to-do list is a long list of activities that roll on from one day to the next.

What actions do I need to take today to execute on my vision or work strategy?

For those working in a leadership role, this question asks you to consider what you need to action strategically, not tactically. A percentage of your time needs to be allocated to non-operational activities. Sometimes you will not need to action strategic objectives on a daily basis, but you must still remain focused on the big picture. For those not working in a leadership role, you can consider this question in the context of your personal vision. What do you need to do today to take one step closer to fulfilling a personal vision or life goal?

About The Half Reflection

The half reflection is an exercise that asks you to consider the answers and reflections you've composed in response to the prompts given across the last six months. This allows you to track your self mastery journey and note any emerging themes. It is encouraging to see how far we have travelled and also to provide ourselves with a map of sorts, which shows us in which direction our journey is taking us.

I accept that this is my moment;
the only moment I have in my life.

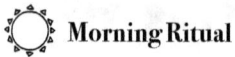 **Morning Ritual**

One thing I can get excited about today is...

....

I am grateful this morning because...

....

The word that best describes the person I want to be today is...

....

One bold action I can take today is...

....

'Coach me' to myself: Today you need to remember that...

....

I would know today is a good day if...

....

☾ Evening Ritual

Tonight I am grateful because...

....

A situation that I handled well today was...

....

Something I learnt today was...

....

I could have made today even better by...

....

One thing I will let go of for tomorrow is...

....

One thing I will commit to tomorrow is...

....

Focus Daily Planner

Date: .... / .... / ....

Affirmation – Today's message to myself:

....
....
....
....

Communication – Who must I communicate with today?

....
....
....

Execution

What tasks must be done today?

....
....
....

What actions do I need to take today to execute on my vision or work strategy?

....
....
....
....
....

 Morning Ritual

One thing I can get excited about today is...

....

I am grateful this morning because...

....

The word that best describes the person I want to be today is...

....

One bold action I can take today is...

....

'Coach me' to myself: Today you need to remember that...

....

I would know today is a good day if...

....

Evening Ritual

Tonight I am grateful because...

....

A situation that I handled well today was...

....

Something I learnt today was...

....

I could have made today even better by...

....

One thing I will let go of for tomorrow is...

....

One thing I will commit to tomorrow is...

....

Focus Daily Planner

Date: .... / .... / ....

Affirmation – Today's message to myself:

....

....

....

....

Communication – Who must I communicate with today?

....

....

....

Execution

What tasks must be done today?

....

....

....

What actions do I need to take today to execute on my vision or work strategy?

....

....

....

....

....

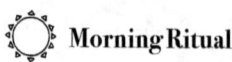 **Morning Ritual**

One thing I can get excited about today is...

....

I am grateful this morning because...

....

The word that best describes the person I want to be today is...

....

One bold action I can take today is...

....

'Coach me' to myself: Today you need to remember that...

....

I would know today is a good day if...

....

☾ Evening Ritual

Tonight I am grateful because...

....

A situation that I handled well today was...

....

Something I learnt today was...

....

I could have made today even better by...

....

One thing I will let go of for tomorrow is...

....

One thing I will commit to tomorrow is...

....

Focus Daily Planner

Date: .... / .... / ....

Affirmation – Today's message to myself:

....
....
....
....

Communication – Who must I communicate with today?

....
....
....

Execution

What tasks must be done today?

....
....
....

What actions do I need to take today to execute on my vision or work strategy?

....
....
....
....
....

☀ Morning Ritual

One thing I can get excited about today is...

....

I am grateful this morning because...

....

The word that best describes the person I want to be today is...

....

One bold action I can take today is...

....

'Coach me' to myself: Today you need to remember that...

....

I would know today is a good day if...

....

☾ Evening Ritual

Tonight I am grateful because...

....

A situation that I handled well today was...

....

Something I learnt today was...

....

I could have made today even better by...

....

One thing I will let go of for tomorrow is...

....

One thing I will commit to tomorrow is...

....

Focus Daily Planner

Date: .... / .... / ....

Affirmation – Today's message to myself:

....

....

....

....

Communication – Who must I communicate with today?

....

....

....

Execution

What tasks must be done today?

....

....

....

What actions do I need to take today to execute on my vision or work strategy?

....

....

....

....

....

☀ Morning Ritual

One thing I can get excited about today is...

....

I am grateful this morning because...

....

The word that best describes the person I want to be today is...

....

One bold action I can take today is...

....

'Coach me' to myself: Today you need to remember that...

....

I would know today is a good day if...

....

☾ Evening Ritual

Tonight I am grateful because...

....

A situation that I handled well today was...

....

Something I learnt today was...

....

I could have made today even better by...

....

One thing I will let go of for tomorrow is...

....

One thing I will commit to tomorrow is...

....

Focus Daily Planner

Date: .... / .... / ....

Affirmation – Today's message to myself:

....
....
....
....

Communication – Who must I communicate with today?

....
....
....

Execution

What tasks must be done today?

....
....
....

What actions do I need to take today to execute on my vision or work strategy?

....
....
....
....
....

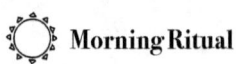 **Morning Ritual**

One thing I can get excited about today is...

....

I am grateful this morning because...

....

The word that best describes the person I want to be today is...

....

One bold action I can take today is...

....

'Coach me' to myself: Today you need to remember that...

....

I would know today is a good day if...

....

Evening Ritual

Tonight I am grateful because...

....

A situation that I handled well today was...

....

Something I learnt today was...

....

I could have made today even better by...

....

One thing I will let go of for tomorrow is...

....

One thing I will commit to tomorrow is...

....

Focus Daily Planner

Date: .... / .... / ....

Affirmation – Today's message to myself:

....
....
....
....

Communication – Who must I communicate with today?

....
....
....

Execution

What tasks must be done today?

....
....
....

What actions do I need to take today to execute on my vision or work strategy?

....
....
....
....
....

 Morning Ritual

One thing I can get excited about today is...

....

I am grateful this morning because...

....

The word that best describes the person I want to be today is...

....

One bold action I can take today is...

....

'Coach me' to myself: Today you need to remember that...

....

I would know today is a good day if...

....

Evening Ritual

Tonight I am grateful because...

....

A situation that I handled well today was...

....

Something I learnt today was...

....

I could have made today even better by...

....

One thing I will let go of for tomorrow is...

....

One thing I will commit to tomorrow is...

....

Focus Daily Planner

Date: .... / .... / ....

Affirmation – Today's message to myself:

....

....

....

....

Communication – Who must I communicate with today?

....

....

....

Execution

What tasks must be done today?

....

....

....

What actions do I need to take today to execute on my vision or work strategy?

....

....

....

....

....

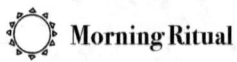 **Morning Ritual**

One thing I can get excited about today is...

....

I am grateful this morning because...

....

The word that best describes the person I want to be today is...

....

One bold action I can take today is...

....

'Coach me' to myself: Today you need to remember that...

....

I would know today is a good day if...

....

Evening Ritual

Tonight I am grateful because...

....

A situation that I handled well today was...

....

Something I learnt today was...

....

I could have made today even better by...

....

One thing I will let go of for tomorrow is...

....

One thing I will commit to tomorrow is...

....

Focus Daily Planner

Date: .... / .... / ....

Affirmation – Today's message to myself:

....

....

....

....

Communication – Who must I communicate with today?

....

....

....

Execution

What tasks must be done today?

....

....

....

What actions do I need to take today to execute on my vision or work strategy?

....

....

....

....

....

 Morning Ritual

One thing I can get excited about today is...

....

I am grateful this morning because...

....

The word that best describes the person I want to be today is...

....

One bold action I can take today is...

....

'Coach me' to myself: Today you need to remember that...

....

I would know today is a good day if...

....

☾ Evening Ritual

Tonight I am grateful because...

....

A situation that I handled well today was...

....

Something I learnt today was...

....

I could have made today even better by...

....

One thing I will let go of for tomorrow is...

....

One thing I will commit to tomorrow is...

....

Focus Daily Planner

Date: .... / .... / ....

Affirmation – Today's message to myself:

....
....
....
....

Communication – Who must I communicate with today?

....
....
....

Execution

What tasks must be done today?

....
....
....

What actions do I need to take today to execute on my vision or work strategy?

....
....
....
....
....

 **Morning Ritual**

One thing I can get excited about today is...

....

I am grateful this morning because...

....

The word that best describes the person I want to be today is...

....

One bold action I can take today is...

....

'Coach me' to myself: Today you need to remember that...

....

I would know today is a good day if...

....

Evening Ritual

Tonight I am grateful because...

....

A situation that I handled well today was...

....

Something I learnt today was...

....

I could have made today even better by...

....

One thing I will let go of for tomorrow is...

....

One thing I will commit to tomorrow is...

....

Focus Daily Planner

Date: .... / .... / ....

Affirmation – Today's message to myself:

....

....

....

....

Communication – Who must I communicate with today?

....

....

....

Execution

What tasks must be done today?

....

....

....

What actions do I need to take today to execute on my vision or work strategy?

....

....

....

....

....

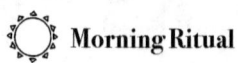 Morning Ritual

One thing I can get excited about today is…

....

I am grateful this morning because…

....

The word that best describes the person I want to be today is…

....

One bold action I can take today is…

....

'Coach me' to myself: Today you need to remember that…

....

I would know today is a good day if…

....

Evening Ritual

Tonight I am grateful because…

....

A situation that I handled well today was…

....

Something I learnt today was…

....

I could have made today even better by…

....

One thing I will let go of for tomorrow is…

....

One thing I will commit to tomorrow is…

....

Focus Daily Planner

Date: .... / .... / ....

Affirmation – Today's message to myself:

....
....
....
....

Communication – Who must I communicate with today?

....
....
....

Execution

What tasks must be done today?

....
....
....

What actions do I need to take today to execute on my vision or work strategy?

....
....
....
....
....

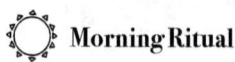 Morning Ritual

One thing I can get excited about today is...

....

I am grateful this morning because...

....

The word that best describes the person I want to be today is...

....

One bold action I can take today is...

....

'Coach me' to myself: Today you need to remember that...

....

I would know today is a good day if...

....

☾ Evening Ritual

Tonight I am grateful because...

....

A situation that I handled well today was...

....

Something I learnt today was...

....

I could have made today even better by...

....

One thing I will let go of for tomorrow is...

....

One thing I will commit to tomorrow is...

....

Focus Daily Planner

Date: ………… / ………… / …………

Affirmation – Today's message to myself:

....

....

....

....

Communication – Who must I communicate with today?

....

....

....

Execution

What tasks must be done today?

....

....

....

What actions do I need to take today to execute on my vision or work strategy?

....

....

....

....

....

☼ Morning Ritual

One thing I can get excited about today is...

....

I am grateful this morning because...

....

The word that best describes the person I want to be today is...

....

One bold action I can take today is...

....

'Coach me' to myself: Today you need to remember that...

....

I would know today is a good day if...

....

☾ Evening Ritual

Tonight I am grateful because...

....

A situation that I handled well today was...

....

Something I learnt today was...

....

I could have made today even better by...

....

One thing I will let go of for tomorrow is...

....

One thing I will commit to tomorrow is...

....

Focus Daily Planner

Date: .... / .... / ....

Affirmation – Today's message to myself:

....
....
....
....

Communication – Who must I communicate with today?

....
....
....

Execution

What tasks must be done today?

....
....
....

What actions do I need to take today to execute on my vision or work strategy?

....
....
....
....
....

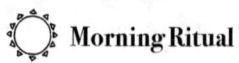 Morning Ritual

One thing I can get excited about today is...

....

I am grateful this morning because...

....

The word that best describes the person I want to be today is...

....

One bold action I can take today is...

....

'Coach me' to myself: Today you need to remember that...

....

I would know today is a good day if...

....

Evening Ritual

Tonight I am grateful because...

....

A situation that I handled well today was...

....

Something I learnt today was...

....

I could have made today even better by...

....

One thing I will let go of for tomorrow is...

....

One thing I will commit to tomorrow is...

....

Focus Daily Planner

Date: .... / .... / ....

Affirmation – Today's message to myself:

....

....

....

....

Communication – Who must I communicate with today?

....

....

....

Execution

What tasks must be done today?

....

....

....

What actions do I need to take today to execute on my vision or work strategy?

....

....

....

....

....

 **Morning Ritual**

One thing I can get excited about today is...

....

I am grateful this morning because...

....

The word that best describes the person I want to be today is...

....

One bold action I can take today is...

....

'Coach me' to myself: Today you need to remember that...

....

I would know today is a good day if...

....

☾ Evening Ritual

Tonight I am grateful because...

....

A situation that I handled well today was...

....

Something I learnt today was...

....

I could have made today even better by...

....

One thing I will let go of for tomorrow is...

....

One thing I will commit to tomorrow is...

....

Focus Daily Planner

Date: .... / .... / ....

Affirmation – Today's message to myself:

....

....

....

....

Communication – Who must I communicate with today?

....

....

....

Execution

What tasks must be done today?

....

....

....

What actions do I need to take today to execute on my vision or work strategy?

....

....

....

....

....

 Morning Ritual

One thing I can get excited about today is...

....

I am grateful this morning because...

....

The word that best describes the person I want to be today is...

....

One bold action I can take today is...

....

'Coach me' to myself: Today you need to remember that...

....

I would know today is a good day if...

....

Evening Ritual

Tonight I am grateful because...

....

A situation that I handled well today was...

....

Something I learnt today was...

....

I could have made today even better by...

....

One thing I will let go of for tomorrow is...

....

One thing I will commit to tomorrow is...

....

Focus Daily Planner

Date: .... / .... / ....

Affirmation – Today's message to myself:

....

....

....

....

Communication – Who must I communicate with today?

....

....

....

Execution

What tasks must be done today?

....

....

....

What actions do I need to take today to execute on my vision or work strategy?

....

....

....

....

....

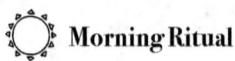 Morning Ritual

One thing I can get excited about today is…

....

I am grateful this morning because…

....

The word that best describes the person I want to be today is…

....

One bold action I can take today is…

....

'Coach me' to myself: Today you need to remember that…

....

I would know today is a good day if…

....

Evening Ritual

Tonight I am grateful because…

....

A situation that I handled well today was…

....

Something I learnt today was…

....

I could have made today even better by…

....

One thing I will let go of for tomorrow is…

....

One thing I will commit to tomorrow is…

....

Focus Daily Planner

Date: .... / .... / ....

Affirmation – Today's message to myself:

....

....

....

....

Communication – Who must I communicate with today?

....

....

....

Execution

What tasks must be done today?

....

....

....

What actions do I need to take today to execute on my vision or work strategy?

....

....

....

....

....

 Morning Ritual

One thing I can get excited about today is...

....

I am grateful this morning because...

....

The word that best describes the person I want to be today is...

....

One bold action I can take today is...

....

'Coach me' to myself: Today you need to remember that...

....

I would know today is a good day if...

....

☾ Evening Ritual

Tonight I am grateful because...

....

A situation that I handled well today was...

....

Something I learnt today was...

....

I could have made today even better by...

....

One thing I will let go of for tomorrow is...

....

One thing I will commit to tomorrow is...

....

Focus Daily Planner

Date: .... / .... / ....

Affirmation – Today's message to myself:

....

....

....

....

Communication – Who must I communicate with today?

....

....

....

Execution

What tasks must be done today?

....

....

....

What actions do I need to take today to execute on my vision or work strategy?

....

....

....

....

....

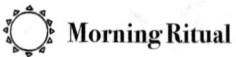 **Morning Ritual**

One thing I can get excited about today is...

....

I am grateful this morning because...

....

The word that best describes the person I want to be today is...

....

One bold action I can take today is...

....

'Coach me' to myself: Today you need to remember that...

....

I would know today is a good day if...

....

☾ Evening Ritual

Tonight I am grateful because...

....

A situation that I handled well today was...

....

Something I learnt today was...

....

I could have made today even better by...

....

One thing I will let go of for tomorrow is...

....

One thing I will commit to tomorrow is...

....

Focus Daily Planner

Date: .... / .... / ....

Affirmation – Today's message to myself:

....

....

....

....

Communication – Who must I communicate with today?

....

....

....

Execution

What tasks must be done today?

....

....

....

What actions do I need to take today to execute on my vision or work strategy?

....

....

....

....

....

 **Morning Ritual**

One thing I can get excited about today is...

....

I am grateful this morning because...

....

The word that best describes the person I want to be today is...

....

One bold action I can take today is...

....

'Coach me' to myself: Today you need to remember that...

....

I would know today is a good day if...

....

☾ Evening Ritual

Tonight I am grateful because...

....

A situation that I handled well today was...

....

Something I learnt today was...

....

I could have made today even better by...

....

One thing I will let go of for tomorrow is...

....

One thing I will commit to tomorrow is...

....

Focus Daily Planner

Date: .... / .... / ....

Affirmation – Today's message to myself:

....

....

....

....

Communication – Who must I communicate with today?

....

....

....

Execution

What tasks must be done today?

....

....

....

What actions do I need to take today to execute on my vision or work strategy?

....

....

....

....

....

 Morning Ritual

One thing I can get excited about today is...
....

I am grateful this morning because...
....

The word that best describes the person I want to be today is...
....

One bold action I can take today is...
....

'Coach me' to myself: Today you need to remember that...
....

I would know today is a good day if...
....

Evening Ritual

Tonight I am grateful because...
....

A situation that I handled well today was...
....

Something I learnt today was...
....

I could have made today even better by...
....

One thing I will let go of for tomorrow is...
....

One thing I will commit to tomorrow is...
....

Focus Daily Planner

Date: .... / .... / ....

Affirmation – Today's message to myself:

....

....

....

....

Communication – Who must I communicate with today?

....

....

....

Execution

What tasks must be done today?

....

....

....

What actions do I need to take today to execute on my vision or work strategy?

....

....

....

....

....

☼ Morning Ritual

One thing I can get excited about today is...

....

I am grateful this morning because...

....

The word that best describes the person I want to be today is...

....

One bold action I can take today is...

....

'Coach me' to myself: Today you need to remember that...

....

I would know today is a good day if...

....

☽ Evening Ritual

Tonight I am grateful because...

....

A situation that I handled well today was...

....

Something I learnt today was...

....

I could have made today even better by...

....

One thing I will let go of for tomorrow is...

....

One thing I will commit to tomorrow is...

....

Focus Daily Planner

Date: .... / .... / ....

Affirmation – Today's message to myself:

....
....
....
....

Communication – Who must I communicate with today?

....
....
....

Execution

What tasks must be done today?

....
....
....

What actions do I need to take today to execute on my vision or work strategy?

....
....
....
....
....

 **Morning Ritual**

One thing I can get excited about today is…
....

I am grateful this morning because…
....

The word that best describes the person I want to be today is…
....

One bold action I can take today is…
....

'Coach me' to myself: Today you need to remember that…
....

I would know today is a good day if…
....

Evening Ritual

Tonight I am grateful because…
....

A situation that I handled well today was…
....

Something I learnt today was…
....

I could have made today even better by…
....

One thing I will let go of for tomorrow is…
....

One thing I will commit to tomorrow is…
....

Focus Daily Planner

Date: .... / .... / ....

Affirmation – Today's message to myself:

....

....

....

....

Communication – Who must I communicate with today?

....

....

....

Execution

What tasks must be done today?

....

....

....

What actions do I need to take today to execute on my vision or work strategy?

....

....

....

....

....

 **Morning Ritual**

One thing I can get excited about today is...

....

I am grateful this morning because...

....

The word that best describes the person I want to be today is...

....

One bold action I can take today is...

....

'Coach me' to myself: Today you need to remember that...

....

I would know today is a good day if...

....

Evening Ritual

Tonight I am grateful because...

....

A situation that I handled well today was...

....

Something I learnt today was...

....

I could have made today even better by...

....

One thing I will let go of for tomorrow is...

....

One thing I will commit to tomorrow is...

....

Focus Daily Planner

Date: .... / .... / ....

Affirmation – Today's message to myself:

....
....
....
....

Communication – Who must I communicate with today?

....
....
....

Execution

What tasks must be done today?

....
....
....

What actions do I need to take today to execute on my vision or work strategy?

....
....
....
....
....

 **Morning Ritual**

One thing I can get excited about today is...

....

I am grateful this morning because...

....

The word that best describes the person I want to be today is...

....

One bold action I can take today is...

....

'Coach me' to myself: Today you need to remember that...

....

I would know today is a good day if...

....

☾ Evening Ritual

Tonight I am grateful because...

....

A situation that I handled well today was...

....

Something I learnt today was...

....

I could have made today even better by...

....

One thing I will let go of for tomorrow is...

....

One thing I will commit to tomorrow is...

....

Focus Daily Planner

Date: .... / .... / ....

Affirmation – Today's message to myself:

....

....

....

....

Communication – Who must I communicate with today?

....

....

....

Execution

What tasks must be done today?

....

....

....

What actions do I need to take today to execute on my vision or work strategy?

....

....

....

....

....

 Morning Ritual

One thing I can get excited about today is...

....

I am grateful this morning because...

....

The word that best describes the person I want to be today is...

....

One bold action I can take today is...

....

'Coach me' to myself: Today you need to remember that...

....

I would know today is a good day if...

....

☾ Evening Ritual

Tonight I am grateful because...

....

A situation that I handled well today was...

....

Something I learnt today was...

....

I could have made today even better by...

....

One thing I will let go of for tomorrow is...

....

One thing I will commit to tomorrow is...

....

Focus Daily Planner

Date: .... / .... / ....

Affirmation – Today's message to myself:

....

....

....

....

Communication – Who must I communicate with today?

....

....

....

Execution

What tasks must be done today?

....

....

....

What actions do I need to take today to execute on my vision or work strategy?

....

....

....

....

....

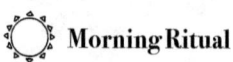 **Morning Ritual**

One thing I can get excited about today is...

....

I am grateful this morning because...

....

The word that best describes the person I want to be today is...

....

One bold action I can take today is...

....

'Coach me' to myself: Today you need to remember that...

....

I would know today is a good day if...

....

☾ Evening Ritual

Tonight I am grateful because...

....

A situation that I handled well today was...

....

Something I learnt today was...

....

I could have made today even better by...

....

One thing I will let go of for tomorrow is...

....

One thing I will commit to tomorrow is...

....

Focus Daily Planner

Date: .... / .... / ....

Affirmation – Today's message to myself:

....
....
....
....

Communication – Who must I communicate with today?

....
....
....

Execution

What tasks must be done today?

....
....
....

What actions do I need to take today to execute on my vision or work strategy?

....
....
....
....
....

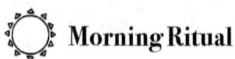 Morning Ritual

One thing I can get excited about today is...

....

I am grateful this morning because...

....

The word that best describes the person I want to be today is...

....

One bold action I can take today is...

....

'Coach me' to myself: Today you need to remember that...

....

I would know today is a good day if...

....

Evening Ritual

Tonight I am grateful because...

....

A situation that I handled well today was...

....

Something I learnt today was...

....

I could have made today even better by...

....

One thing I will let go of for tomorrow is...

....

One thing I will commit to tomorrow is...

....

Focus Daily Planner

Date: .... / .... / ....

Affirmation – Today's message to myself:

....

....

....

....

Communication – Who must I communicate with today?

....

....

....

Execution

What tasks must be done today?

....

....

....

What actions do I need to take today to execute on my vision or work strategy?

....

....

....

....

....

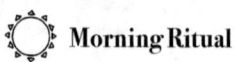 Morning Ritual

One thing I can get excited about today is...

....

I am grateful this morning because...

....

The word that best describes the person I want to be today is...

....

One bold action I can take today is...

....

'Coach me' to myself: Today you need to remember that...

....

I would know today is a good day if...

....

Evening Ritual

Tonight I am grateful because...

....

A situation that I handled well today was...

....

Something I learnt today was...

....

I could have made today even better by...

....

One thing I will let go of for tomorrow is...

....

One thing I will commit to tomorrow is...

....

Focus Daily Planner

Date: .... / .... / ....

Affirmation – Today's message to myself:

....

....

....

....

Communication – Who must I communicate with today?

....

....

....

Execution

What tasks must be done today?

....

....

....

What actions do I need to take today to execute on my vision or work strategy?

....

....

....

....

....

 Morning Ritual

One thing I can get excited about today is...
....

I am grateful this morning because...
....

The word that best describes the person I want to be today is...
....

One bold action I can take today is...
....

'Coach me' to myself: Today you need to remember that...
....

I would know today is a good day if...
....

☾ Evening Ritual

Tonight I am grateful because...
....

A situation that I handled well today was...
....

Something I learnt today was...
....

I could have made today even better by...
....

One thing I will let go of for tomorrow is...
....

One thing I will commit to tomorrow is...
....

Focus Daily Planner

Date: .... / .... / ....

Affirmation – Today's message to myself:

....

....

....

....

Communication – Who must I communicate with today?

....

....

....

Execution

What tasks must be done today?

....

....

....

What actions do I need to take today to execute on my vision or work strategy?

....

....

....

....

....

 **Morning Ritual**

One thing I can get excited about today is...

....

I am grateful this morning because...

....

The word that best describes the person I want to be today is...

....

One bold action I can take today is...

....

'Coach me' to myself: Today you need to remember that...

....

I would know today is a good day if...

....

Evening Ritual

Tonight I am grateful because...

....

A situation that I handled well today was...

....

Something I learnt today was...

....

I could have made today even better by...

....

One thing I will let go of for tomorrow is...

....

One thing I will commit to tomorrow is...

....

Focus Daily Planner

Date: .... / .... / ....

Affirmation – Today's message to myself:

....
....
....
....

Communication – Who must I communicate with today?

....
....
....

Execution

What tasks must be done today?

....
....
....

What actions do I need to take today to execute on my vision or work strategy?

....
....
....
....
....

 Morning Ritual

One thing I can get excited about today is...

....

I am grateful this morning because...

....

The word that best describes the person I want to be today is...

....

One bold action I can take today is...

....

'Coach me' to myself: Today you need to remember that...

....

I would know today is a good day if...

....

Evening Ritual

Tonight I am grateful because...

....

A situation that I handled well today was...

....

Something I learnt today was...

....

I could have made today even better by...

....

One thing I will let go of for tomorrow is...

....

One thing I will commit to tomorrow is...

....

Focus Daily Planner

Date: .... / .... / ....

Affirmation – Today's message to myself:

....
....
....
....

Communication – Who must I communicate with today?

....
....
....

Execution

What tasks must be done today?

....
....
....

What actions do I need to take today to execute on my vision or work strategy?

....
....
....
....
....

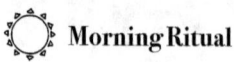 Morning Ritual

One thing I can get excited about today is...

....

I am grateful this morning because...

....

The word that best describes the person I want to be today is...

....

One bold action I can take today is...

....

'Coach me' to myself: Today you need to remember that...

....

I would know today is a good day if...

....

Evening Ritual

Tonight I am grateful because...

....

A situation that I handled well today was...

....

Something I learnt today was...

....

I could have made today even better by...

....

One thing I will let go of for tomorrow is...

....

One thing I will commit to tomorrow is...

....

Focus Daily Planner

Date: .... / .... / ....

Affirmation – Today's message to myself:

....

....

....

....

Communication – Who must I communicate with today?

....

....

....

Execution

What tasks must be done today?

....

....

....

What actions do I need to take today to execute on my vision or work strategy?

....

....

....

....

....

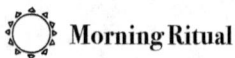 ## Morning Ritual

One thing I can get excited about today is...

....

I am grateful this morning because...

....

The word that best describes the person I want to be today is...

....

One bold action I can take today is...

....

'Coach me' to myself: Today you need to remember that...

....

I would know today is a good day if...

....

Evening Ritual

Tonight I am grateful because...

....

A situation that I handled well today was...

....

Something I learnt today was...

....

I could have made today even better by...

....

One thing I will let go of for tomorrow is...

....

One thing I will commit to tomorrow is...

....

Focus Daily Planner

Date: .... / .... / ....

Affirmation – Today's message to myself:

....

....

....

....

Communication – Who must I communicate with today?

....

....

....

Execution

What tasks must be done today?

....

....

....

What actions do I need to take today to execute on my vision or work strategy?

....

....

....

....

....

 **Morning Ritual**

One thing I can get excited about today is...

....

I am grateful this morning because...

....

The word that best describes the person I want to be today is...

....

One bold action I can take today is...

....

'Coach me' to myself: Today you need to remember that...

....

I would know today is a good day if...

....

☾ Evening Ritual

Tonight I am grateful because...

....

A situation that I handled well today was...

....

Something I learnt today was...

....

I could have made today even better by...

....

One thing I will let go of for tomorrow is...

....

One thing I will commit to tomorrow is...

....

Focus Daily Planner

Date: .... / .... / ....

Affirmation – Today's message to myself:

....

....

....

....

Communication – Who must I communicate with today?

....

....

....

👁 Execution

What tasks must be done today?

....

....

....

What actions do I need to take today to execute on my vision or work strategy?

....

....

....

....

....

 **Morning Ritual**

One thing I can get excited about today is...

....

I am grateful this morning because...

....

The word that best describes the person I want to be today is...

....

One bold action I can take today is...

....

'Coach me' to myself: Today you need to remember that...

....

I would know today is a good day if...

....

☾ Evening Ritual

Tonight I am grateful because...

....

A situation that I handled well today was...

....

Something I learnt today was...

....

I could have made today even better by...

....

One thing I will let go of for tomorrow is...

....

One thing I will commit to tomorrow is...

....

Focus Daily Planner

Date: ………… / ………… / …………

Affirmation – Today's message to myself:

....

....

....

....

Communication – Who must I communicate with today?

....

....

....

Execution

What tasks must be done today?

....

....

....

What actions do I need to take today to execute on my vision or work strategy?

....

....

....

....

....

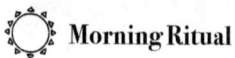 **Morning Ritual**

One thing I can get excited about today is...

....

I am grateful this morning because...

....

The word that best describes the person I want to be today is...

....

One bold action I can take today is...

....

'Coach me' to myself: Today you need to remember that...

....

I would know today is a good day if...

....

Evening Ritual

Tonight I am grateful because...

....

A situation that I handled well today was...

....

Something I learnt today was...

....

I could have made today even better by...

....

One thing I will let go of for tomorrow is...

....

One thing I will commit to tomorrow is...

....

Focus Daily Planner

Date: ………… / ………… / …………

Affirmation – Today's message to myself:

....

....

....

....

Communication – Who must I communicate with today?

....

....

....

Execution

What tasks must be done today?

....

....

....

What actions do I need to take today to execute on my vision or work strategy?

....

....

....

....

....

☀ Morning Ritual

One thing I can get excited about today is...

....

I am grateful this morning because...

....

The word that best describes the person I want to be today is...

....

One bold action I can take today is...

....

'Coach me' to myself: Today you need to remember that...

....

I would know today is a good day if...

....

☾ Evening Ritual

Tonight I am grateful because...

....

A situation that I handled well today was...

....

Something I learnt today was...

....

I could have made today even better by...

....

One thing I will let go of for tomorrow is...

....

One thing I will commit to tomorrow is...

....

Focus Daily Planner

Date: .... / .... / ....

Affirmation – Today's message to myself:

....

....

....

....

Communication – Who must I communicate with today?

....

....

....

Execution

What tasks must be done today?

....

....

....

What actions do I need to take today to execute on my vision or work strategy?

....

....

....

....

....

 ## Morning Ritual

One thing I can get excited about today is...

....

I am grateful this morning because...

....

The word that best describes the person I want to be today is...

....

One bold action I can take today is...

....

'Coach me' to myself: Today you need to remember that...

....

I would know today is a good day if...

....

Evening Ritual

Tonight I am grateful because...

....

A situation that I handled well today was...

....

Something I learnt today was...

....

I could have made today even better by...

....

One thing I will let go of for tomorrow is...

....

One thing I will commit to tomorrow is...

....

Focus Daily Planner

Date: .... / .... / ....

Affirmation – Today's message to myself:

....
....
....
....

Communication – Who must I communicate with today?

....
....
....

Execution

What tasks must be done today?

....
....
....

What actions do I need to take today to execute on my vision or work strategy?

....
....
....
....
....

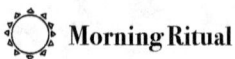 **Morning Ritual**

One thing I can get excited about today is...

....

I am grateful this morning because...

....

The word that best describes the person I want to be today is...

....

One bold action I can take today is...

....

'Coach me' to myself: Today you need to remember that...

....

I would know today is a good day if...

....

☾ Evening Ritual

Tonight I am grateful because...

....

A situation that I handled well today was...

....

Something I learnt today was...

....

I could have made today even better by...

....

One thing I will let go of for tomorrow is...

....

One thing I will commit to tomorrow is...

....

Focus Daily Planner

Date: .... / .... / ....

Affirmation – Today's message to myself:

....

....

....

....

Communication – Who must I communicate with today?

....

....

....

Execution

What tasks must be done today?

....

....

....

What actions do I need to take today to execute on my vision or work strategy?

....

....

....

....

....

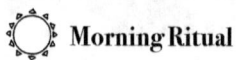 Morning Ritual

One thing I can get excited about today is…

....

I am grateful this morning because…

....

The word that best describes the person I want to be today is…

....

One bold action I can take today is…

....

'Coach me' to myself: Today you need to remember that…

....

I would know today is a good day if…

....

☾ Evening Ritual

Tonight I am grateful because…

....

A situation that I handled well today was…

....

Something I learnt today was…

....

I could have made today even better by…

....

One thing I will let go of for tomorrow is…

....

One thing I will commit to tomorrow is…

....

Focus Daily Planner

Date: .... / .... / ....

Affirmation – Today's message to myself:

....

....

....

....

Communication – Who must I communicate with today?

....

....

....

Execution

What tasks must be done today?

....

....

....

What actions do I need to take today to execute on my vision or work strategy?

....

....

....

....

....

 Morning Ritual

One thing I can get excited about today is...

....

I am grateful this morning because...

....

The word that best describes the person I want to be today is...

....

One bold action I can take today is...

....

'Coach me' to myself: Today you need to remember that...

....

I would know today is a good day if...

....

☾ Evening Ritual

Tonight I am grateful because...

....

A situation that I handled well today was...

....

Something I learnt today was...

....

I could have made today even better by...

....

One thing I will let go of for tomorrow is...

....

One thing I will commit to tomorrow is...

....

Focus Daily Planner

Date: .... / .... / ....

Affirmation – Today's message to myself:

....
....
....
....

Communication – Who must I communicate with today?

....
....
....

Execution

What tasks must be done today?

....
....
....

What actions do I need to take today to execute on my vision or work strategy?

....
....
....
....
....

☼ Morning Ritual

One thing I can get excited about today is...

....

I am grateful this morning because...

....

The word that best describes the person I want to be today is...

....

One bold action I can take today is...

....

'Coach me' to myself: Today you need to remember that...

....

I would know today is a good day if...

....

☾ Evening Ritual

Tonight I am grateful because...

....

A situation that I handled well today was...

....

Something I learnt today was...

....

I could have made today even better by...

....

One thing I will let go of for tomorrow is...

....

One thing I will commit to tomorrow is...

....

Focus Daily Planner

Date: .... / .... / ....

Affirmation – Today's message to myself:

....
....
....
....

Communication – Who must I communicate with today?

....
....
....

Execution

What tasks must be done today?

....
....
....

What actions do I need to take today to execute on my vision or work strategy?

....
....
....
....
....

 Morning Ritual

One thing I can get excited about today is...

....

I am grateful this morning because...

....

The word that best describes the person I want to be today is...

....

One bold action I can take today is...

....

'Coach me' to myself: Today you need to remember that...

....

I would know today is a good day if...

....

☾ Evening Ritual

Tonight I am grateful because...

....

A situation that I handled well today was...

....

Something I learnt today was...

....

I could have made today even better by...

....

One thing I will let go of for tomorrow is...

....

One thing I will commit to tomorrow is...

....

Focus Daily Planner

Date: .... / .... / ....

Affirmation – Today's message to myself:

....

....

....

....

Communication – Who must I communicate with today?

....

....

....

Execution

What tasks must be done today?

....

....

....

What actions do I need to take today to execute on my vision or work strategy?

....

....

....

....

....

 Morning Ritual

One thing I can get excited about today is...

....

I am grateful this morning because...

....

The word that best describes the person I want to be today is...

....

One bold action I can take today is...

....

'Coach me' to myself: Today you need to remember that...

....

I would know today is a good day if...

....

Evening Ritual

Tonight I am grateful because...

....

A situation that I handled well today was...

....

Something I learnt today was...

....

I could have made today even better by...

....

One thing I will let go of for tomorrow is...

....

One thing I will commit to tomorrow is...

....

Focus Daily Planner

Date: .... / .... / ....

Affirmation – Today's message to myself:

....
....
....
....

Communication – Who must I communicate with today?

....
....
....

👁 Execution

What tasks must be done today?

....
....
....

What actions do I need to take today to execute on my vision or work strategy?

....
....
....
....
....

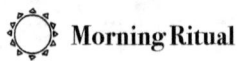 Morning Ritual

One thing I can get excited about today is...

....

I am grateful this morning because...

....

The word that best describes the person I want to be today is...

....

One bold action I can take today is...

....

'Coach me' to myself: Today you need to remember that...

....

I would know today is a good day if...

....

Evening Ritual

Tonight I am grateful because...

....

A situation that I handled well today was...

....

Something I learnt today was...

....

I could have made today even better by...

....

One thing I will let go of for tomorrow is...

....

One thing I will commit to tomorrow is...

....

Focus Daily Planner

Date: .... / .... / ....

Affirmation – Today's message to myself:

....

....

....

....

Communication – Who must I communicate with today?

....

....

....

Execution

What tasks must be done today?

....

....

....

What actions do I need to take today to execute on my vision or work strategy?

....

....

....

....

....

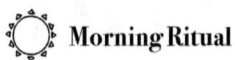 ## Morning Ritual

One thing I can get excited about today is...

....

I am grateful this morning because...

....

The word that best describes the person I want to be today is...

....

One bold action I can take today is...

....

'Coach me' to myself: Today you need to remember that...

....

I would know today is a good day if...

....

Evening Ritual

Tonight I am grateful because...

....

A situation that I handled well today was...

....

Something I learnt today was...

....

I could have made today even better by...

....

One thing I will let go of for tomorrow is...

....

One thing I will commit to tomorrow is...

....

Focus Daily Planner

Date: ………… / ………… / …………

Affirmation – Today's message to myself:

....

....

....

....

Communication – Who must I communicate with today?

....

....

....

Execution

What tasks must be done today?

....

....

....

What actions do I need to take today to execute on my vision or work strategy?

....

....

....

....

....

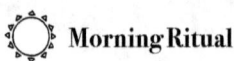 Morning Ritual

One thing I can get excited about today is…

....

I am grateful this morning because…

....

The word that best describes the person I want to be today is…

....

One bold action I can take today is…

....

'Coach me' to myself: Today you need to remember that…

....

I would know today is a good day if…

....

☾ Evening Ritual

Tonight I am grateful because…

....

A situation that I handled well today was…

....

Something I learnt today was…

....

I could have made today even better by…

....

One thing I will let go of for tomorrow is…

....

One thing I will commit to tomorrow is…

....

Focus Daily Planner

Date: .... / .... / ....

Affirmation – Today's message to myself:

....
....
....
....

Communication – Who must I communicate with today?

....
....
....

Execution

What tasks must be done today?

....
....
....

What actions do I need to take today to execute on my vision or work strategy?

....
....
....
....
....

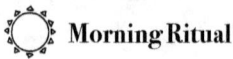 Morning Ritual

One thing I can get excited about today is...

....

I am grateful this morning because...

....

The word that best describes the person I want to be today is...

....

One bold action I can take today is...

....

'Coach me' to myself: Today you need to remember that...

....

I would know today is a good day if...

....

Evening Ritual

Tonight I am grateful because...

....

A situation that I handled well today was...

....

Something I learnt today was...

....

I could have made today even better by...

....

One thing I will let go of for tomorrow is...

....

One thing I will commit to tomorrow is...

....

Focus Daily Planner

Date: .... / .... / ....

Affirmation – Today's message to myself:

....
....
....
....

Communication – Who must I communicate with today?

....
....
....

👁 Execution

What tasks must be done today?

....
....
....

What actions do I need to take today to execute on my vision or work strategy?

....
....
....
....
....

 **Morning Ritual**

One thing I can get excited about today is...

....

I am grateful this morning because...

....

The word that best describes the person I want to be today is...

....

One bold action I can take today is...

....

'Coach me' to myself: Today you need to remember that...

....

I would know today is a good day if...

....

☾ Evening Ritual

Tonight I am grateful because...

....

A situation that I handled well today was...

....

Something I learnt today was...

....

I could have made today even better by...

....

One thing I will let go of for tomorrow is...

....

One thing I will commit to tomorrow is...

....

Focus Daily Planner

Date: .... / .... / ....

Affirmation – Today's message to myself:

....

....

....

....

Communication – Who must I communicate with today?

....

....

....

Execution

What tasks must be done today?

....

....

....

What actions do I need to take today to execute on my vision or work strategy?

....

....

....

....

....

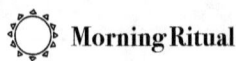 Morning Ritual

One thing I can get excited about today is...

....

I am grateful this morning because...

....

The word that best describes the person I want to be today is...

....

One bold action I can take today is...

....

'Coach me' to myself: Today you need to remember that...

....

I would know today is a good day if...

....

☾ Evening Ritual

Tonight I am grateful because...

....

A situation that I handled well today was...

....

Something I learnt today was...

....

I could have made today even better by...

....

One thing I will let go of for tomorrow is...

....

One thing I will commit to tomorrow is...

....

Focus Daily Planner

Date: ………… / ………… / …………

Affirmation – Today's message to myself:

....

....

....

....

Communication – Who must I communicate with today?

....

....

....

Execution

What tasks must be done today?

....

....

....

What actions do I need to take today to execute on my vision or work strategy?

....

....

....

....

....

 Morning Ritual

One thing I can get excited about today is...

....

I am grateful this morning because...

....

The word that best describes the person I want to be today is...

....

One bold action I can take today is...

....

'Coach me' to myself: Today you need to remember that...

....

I would know today is a good day if...

....

Evening Ritual

Tonight I am grateful because...

....

A situation that I handled well today was...

....

Something I learnt today was...

....

I could have made today even better by...

....

One thing I will let go of for tomorrow is...

....

One thing I will commit to tomorrow is...

....

Focus Daily Planner

Date: .... / .... / ....

Affirmation – Today's message to myself:

....
....
....
....

Communication – Who must I communicate with today?

....
....
....

Execution

What tasks must be done today?

....
....
....

What actions do I need to take today to execute on my vision or work strategy?

....
....
....
....
....

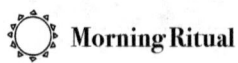 **Morning Ritual**

One thing I can get excited about today is...

....

I am grateful this morning because...

....

The word that best describes the person I want to be today is...

....

One bold action I can take today is...

....

'Coach me' to myself: Today you need to remember that...

....

I would know today is a good day if...

....

☾ Evening Ritual

Tonight I am grateful because...

....

A situation that I handled well today was...

....

Something I learnt today was...

....

I could have made today even better by...

....

One thing I will let go of for tomorrow is...

....

One thing I will commit to tomorrow is...

....

Focus Daily Planner

Date: .... / .... / ....

Affirmation – Today's message to myself:

....
....
....
....

Communication – Who must I communicate with today?

....
....
....

Execution

What tasks must be done today?

....
....
....

What actions do I need to take today to execute on my vision or work strategy?

....
....
....
....
....

 Morning Ritual

One thing I can get excited about today is...

....

I am grateful this morning because...

....

The word that best describes the person I want to be today is...

....

One bold action I can take today is...

....

'Coach me' to myself: Today you need to remember that...

....

I would know today is a good day if...

....

☾ Evening Ritual

Tonight I am grateful because...

....

A situation that I handled well today was...

....

Something I learnt today was...

....

I could have made today even better by...

....

One thing I will let go of for tomorrow is...

....

One thing I will commit to tomorrow is...

....

Focus Daily Planner

Date: .... / .... / ....

Affirmation – Today's message to myself:

....

....

....

....

Communication – Who must I communicate with today?

....

....

....

Execution

What tasks must be done today?

....

....

....

What actions do I need to take today to execute on my vision or work strategy?

....

....

....

....

....

 Morning Ritual

One thing I can get excited about today is...

....

I am grateful this morning because...

....

The word that best describes the person I want to be today is...

....

One bold action I can take today is...

....

'Coach me' to myself: Today you need to remember that...

....

I would know today is a good day if...

....

Evening Ritual

Tonight I am grateful because...

....

A situation that I handled well today was...

....

Something I learnt today was...

....

I could have made today even better by...

....

One thing I will let go of for tomorrow is...

....

One thing I will commit to tomorrow is...

....

Focus Daily Planner

Date: .... / .... / ....

Affirmation – Today's message to myself:

....

....

....

....

Communication – Who must I communicate with today?

....

....

....

Execution

What tasks must be done today?

....

....

....

What actions do I need to take today to execute on my vision or work strategy?

....

....

....

....

....

 Morning Ritual

One thing I can get excited about today is…

....

I am grateful this morning because…

....

The word that best describes the person I want to be today is…

....

One bold action I can take today is…

....

'Coach me' to myself: Today you need to remember that…

....

I would know today is a good day if…

....

☾ Evening Ritual

Tonight I am grateful because…

....

A situation that I handled well today was…

....

Something I learnt today was…

....

I could have made today even better by…

....

One thing I will let go of for tomorrow is…

....

One thing I will commit to tomorrow is…

....

Focus Daily Planner

Date: .... / .... / ....

Affirmation – Today's message to myself:

....
....
....
....

Communication – Who must I communicate with today?

....
....
....

Execution

What tasks must be done today?

....
....
....

What actions do I need to take today to execute on my vision or work strategy?

....
....
....
....
....

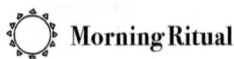 **Morning Ritual**

One thing I can get excited about today is...

....

I am grateful this morning because...

....

The word that best describes the person I want to be today is...

....

One bold action I can take today is...

....

'Coach me' to myself: Today you need to remember that...

....

I would know today is a good day if...

....

☾ Evening Ritual

Tonight I am grateful because...

....

A situation that I handled well today was...

....

Something I learnt today was...

....

I could have made today even better by...

....

One thing I will let go of for tomorrow is...

....

One thing I will commit to tomorrow is...

....

Focus Daily Planner

Date: .... / .... / ....

Affirmation – Today's message to myself:

....

....

....

....

Communication – Who must I communicate with today?

....

....

....

Execution

What tasks must be done today?

....

....

....

What actions do I need to take today to execute on my vision or work strategy?

....

....

....

....

....

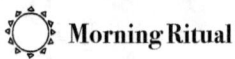
Morning Ritual

One thing I can get excited about today is...

....

I am grateful this morning because...

....

The word that best describes the person I want to be today is...

....

One bold action I can take today is...

....

'Coach me' to myself: Today you need to remember that...

....

I would know today is a good day if...

....

Evening Ritual

Tonight I am grateful because...

....

A situation that I handled well today was...

....

Something I learnt today was...

....

I could have made today even better by...

....

One thing I will let go of for tomorrow is...

....

One thing I will commit to tomorrow is...

....

Focus Daily Planner

Date: .... / .... / ....

Affirmation – Today's message to myself:

....

....

....

....

Communication – Who must I communicate with today?

....

....

....

Execution

What tasks must be done today?

....

....

....

What actions do I need to take today to execute on my vision or work strategy?

....

....

....

....

....

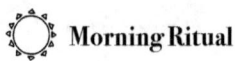 Morning Ritual

One thing I can get excited about today is...

....

I am grateful this morning because...

....

The word that best describes the person I want to be today is...

....

One bold action I can take today is...

....

'Coach me' to myself: Today you need to remember that...

....

I would know today is a good day if...

....

☾ Evening Ritual

Tonight I am grateful because...

....

A situation that I handled well today was...

....

Something I learnt today was...

....

I could have made today even better by...

....

One thing I will let go of for tomorrow is...

....

One thing I will commit to tomorrow is...

....

Focus Daily Planner

Date: .... / .... / ....

Affirmation – Today's message to myself:

....

....

....

....

Communication – Who must I communicate with today?

....

....

....

Execution

What tasks must be done today?

....

....

....

What actions do I need to take today to execute on my vision or work strategy?

....

....

....

....

....

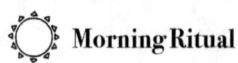 **Morning Ritual**

One thing I can get excited about today is…

....

I am grateful this morning because…

....

The word that best describes the person I want to be today is…

....

One bold action I can take today is…

....

'Coach me' to myself: Today you need to remember that…

....

I would know today is a good day if…

....

☾ Evening Ritual

Tonight I am grateful because…

....

A situation that I handled well today was…

....

Something I learnt today was…

....

I could have made today even better by…

....

One thing I will let go of for tomorrow is…

....

One thing I will commit to tomorrow is…

....

Focus Daily Planner

Date: .... / .... / ....

Affirmation – Today's message to myself:

....
....
....
....

Communication – Who must I communicate with today?

....
....
....

Execution

What tasks must be done today?

....
....
....

What actions do I need to take today to execute on my vision or work strategy?

....
....
....
....
....

 Morning Ritual

One thing I can get excited about today is...

....

I am grateful this morning because...

....

The word that best describes the person I want to be today is...

....

One bold action I can take today is...

....

'Coach me' to myself: Today you need to remember that...

....

I would know today is a good day if...

....

Evening Ritual

Tonight I am grateful because...

....

A situation that I handled well today was...

....

Something I learnt today was...

....

I could have made today even better by...

....

One thing I will let go of for tomorrow is...

....

One thing I will commit to tomorrow is...

....

Focus Daily Planner

Date: .... / .... / ....

Affirmation – Today's message to myself:

....
....
....
....

Communication – Who must I communicate with today?

....
....
....

Execution

What tasks must be done today?

....
....
....

What actions do I need to take today to execute on my vision or work strategy?

....
....
....
....
....

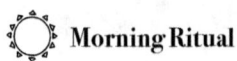 **Morning Ritual**

One thing I can get excited about today is...
....

I am grateful this morning because...
....

The word that best describes the person I want to be today is...
....

One bold action I can take today is...
....

'Coach me' to myself: Today you need to remember that...
....

I would know today is a good day if...
....

☽ Evening Ritual

Tonight I am grateful because...
....

A situation that I handled well today was...
....

Something I learnt today was...
....

I could have made today even better by...
....

One thing I will let go of for tomorrow is...
....

One thing I will commit to tomorrow is...
....

Focus Daily Planner

Date: .... / .... / ....

Affirmation – Today's message to myself:

....

....

....

....

Communication – Who must I communicate with today?

....

....

....

Execution

What tasks must be done today?

....

....

....

What actions do I need to take today to execute on my vision or work strategy?

....

....

....

....

....

 **Morning Ritual**

One thing I can get excited about today is...

....

I am grateful this morning because...

....

The word that best describes the person I want to be today is...

....

One bold action I can take today is...

....

'Coach me' to myself: Today you need to remember that...

....

I would know today is a good day if...

....

☾ Evening Ritual

Tonight I am grateful because...

....

A situation that I handled well today was...

....

Something I learnt today was...

....

I could have made today even better by...

....

One thing I will let go of for tomorrow is...

....

One thing I will commit to tomorrow is...

....

Focus Daily Planner

Date: .... / .... / ....

Affirmation – Today's message to myself:

....
....
....
....

Communication – Who must I communicate with today?

....
....
....

Execution

What tasks must be done today?

....
....
....

What actions do I need to take today to execute on my vision or work strategy?

....
....
....
....
....

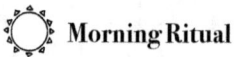 Morning Ritual

One thing I can get excited about today is…

....

I am grateful this morning because…

....

The word that best describes the person I want to be today is…

....

One bold action I can take today is…

....

'Coach me' to myself: Today you need to remember that…

....

I would know today is a good day if…

....

☾ Evening Ritual

Tonight I am grateful because…

....

A situation that I handled well today was…

....

Something I learnt today was…

....

I could have made today even better by…

....

One thing I will let go of for tomorrow is…

....

One thing I will commit to tomorrow is…

....

Focus Daily Planner

Date: .... / .... / ....

Affirmation – Today's message to myself:

....
....
....
....

Communication – Who must I communicate with today?

....
....
....

Execution

What tasks must be done today?

....
....
....

What actions do I need to take today to execute on my vision or work strategy?

....
....
....
....
....

 Morning Ritual

One thing I can get excited about today is…

....

I am grateful this morning because…

....

The word that best describes the person I want to be today is…

....

One bold action I can take today is…

....

'Coach me' to myself: Today you need to remember that…

....

I would know today is a good day if…

....

Evening Ritual

Tonight I am grateful because…

....

A situation that I handled well today was…

....

Something I learnt today was…

....

I could have made today even better by…

....

One thing I will let go of for tomorrow is…

....

One thing I will commit to tomorrow is…

....

Focus Daily Planner

Date: .... / .... / ....

Affirmation – Today's message to myself:

....

....

....

....

Communication – Who must I communicate with today?

....

....

....

👁 Execution

What tasks must be done today?

....

....

....

What actions do I need to take today to execute on my vision or work strategy?

....

....

....

....

....

 Morning Ritual

One thing I can get excited about today is…

....

I am grateful this morning because…

....

The word that best describes the person I want to be today is…

....

One bold action I can take today is…

....

'Coach me' to myself: Today you need to remember that…

....

I would know today is a good day if…

....

☾ Evening Ritual

Tonight I am grateful because…

....

A situation that I handled well today was…

....

Something I learnt today was…

....

I could have made today even better by…

....

One thing I will let go of for tomorrow is…

....

One thing I will commit to tomorrow is…

....

Focus Daily Planner

Date: ………… / ………… / …………

Affirmation – Today's message to myself:

....
....
....
....

Communication – Who must I communicate with today?

....
....
....

Execution

What tasks must be done today?

....
....
....

What actions do I need to take today to execute on my vision or work strategy?

....
....
....
....
....

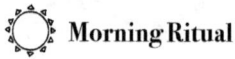 Morning Ritual

One thing I can get excited about today is...

....

I am grateful this morning because...

....

The word that best describes the person I want to be today is...

....

One bold action I can take today is...

....

'Coach me' to myself: Today you need to remember that...

....

I would know today is a good day if...

....

☾ Evening Ritual

Tonight I am grateful because...

....

A situation that I handled well today was...

....

Something I learnt today was...

....

I could have made today even better by...

....

One thing I will let go of for tomorrow is...

....

One thing I will commit to tomorrow is...

....

Focus Daily Planner

Date: .... / .... / ....

Affirmation – Today's message to myself:

....
....
....
....

Communication – Who must I communicate with today?

....
....
....

👁 Execution

What tasks must be done today?

....
....
....

What actions do I need to take today to execute on my vision or work strategy?

....
....
....
....
....

 **Morning Ritual**

One thing I can get excited about today is…
....

I am grateful this morning because…
....

The word that best describes the person I want to be today is…
....

One bold action I can take today is…
....

'Coach me' to myself: Today you need to remember that…
....

I would know today is a good day if…
....

🌙 Evening Ritual

Tonight I am grateful because…
....

A situation that I handled well today was…
....

Something I learnt today was…
....

I could have made today even better by…
....

One thing I will let go of for tomorrow is…
....

One thing I will commit to tomorrow is…
....

Focus Daily Planner

Date: .... / .... / ....

Affirmation – Today's message to myself:

....

....

....

....

Communication – Who must I communicate with today?

....

....

....

Execution

What tasks must be done today?

....

....

....

What actions do I need to take today to execute on my vision or work strategy?

....

....

....

....

....

 Morning Ritual

One thing I can get excited about today is...
....

I am grateful this morning because...
....

The word that best describes the person I want to be today is...
....

One bold action I can take today is...
....

'Coach me' to myself: Today you need to remember that...
....

I would know today is a good day if...
....

Evening Ritual

Tonight I am grateful because...
....

A situation that I handled well today was...
....

Something I learnt today was...
....

I could have made today even better by...
....

One thing I will let go of for tomorrow is...
....

One thing I will commit to tomorrow is...
....

Focus Daily Planner

Date: .... / .... / ....

Affirmation – Today's message to myself:

....
....
....
....

Communication – Who must I communicate with today?

....
....
....

Execution

What tasks must be done today?

....
....
....

What actions do I need to take today to execute on my vision or work strategy?

....
....
....
....
....

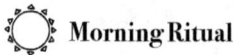 **Morning Ritual**

One thing I can get excited about today is...

....

I am grateful this morning because...

....

The word that best describes the person I want to be today is...

....

One bold action I can take today is...

....

'Coach me' to myself: Today you need to remember that...

....

I would know today is a good day if...

....

Evening Ritual

Tonight I am grateful because...

....

A situation that I handled well today was...

....

Something I learnt today was...

....

I could have made today even better by...

....

One thing I will let go of for tomorrow is...

....

One thing I will commit to tomorrow is...

....

Focus Daily Planner

Date: .... / .... / ....

Affirmation – Today's message to myself:

....

....

....

....

Communication – Who must I communicate with today?

....

....

....

Execution

What tasks must be done today?

....

....

....

What actions do I need to take today to execute on my vision or work strategy?

....

....

....

....

....

☀ Morning Ritual

One thing I can get excited about today is...

....

I am grateful this morning because...

....

The word that best describes the person I want to be today is...

....

One bold action I can take today is...

....

'Coach me' to myself: Today you need to remember that...

....

I would know today is a good day if...

....

☾ Evening Ritual

Tonight I am grateful because...

....

A situation that I handled well today was...

....

Something I learnt today was...

....

I could have made today even better by...

....

One thing I will let go of for tomorrow is...

....

One thing I will commit to tomorrow is...

....

Focus Daily Planner

Date: .... / .... / ....

Affirmation – Today's message to myself:

....
....
....
....

Communication – Who must I communicate with today?

....
....
....

Execution

What tasks must be done today?

....
....
....

What actions do I need to take today to execute on my vision or work strategy?

....
....
....
....
....

 Morning Ritual

One thing I can get excited about today is…

....

I am grateful this morning because…

....

The word that best describes the person I want to be today is…

....

One bold action I can take today is…

....

'Coach me' to myself: Today you need to remember that…

....

I would know today is a good day if…

....

Evening Ritual

Tonight I am grateful because…

....

A situation that I handled well today was…

....

Something I learnt today was…

....

I could have made today even better by…

....

One thing I will let go of for tomorrow is…

....

One thing I will commit to tomorrow is…

....

Focus Daily Planner

Date: .... / .... / ....

Affirmation – Today's message to myself:

....
....
....
....

Communication – Who must I communicate with today?

....
....
....

Execution

What tasks must be done today?

....
....
....

What actions do I need to take today to execute on my vision or work strategy?

....
....
....
....
....

 Morning Ritual

One thing I can get excited about today is...

....

I am grateful this morning because...

....

The word that best describes the person I want to be today is...

....

One bold action I can take today is...

....

'Coach me' to myself: Today you need to remember that...

....

I would know today is a good day if...

....

Evening Ritual

Tonight I am grateful because...

....

A situation that I handled well today was...

....

Something I learnt today was...

....

I could have made today even better by...

....

One thing I will let go of for tomorrow is...

....

One thing I will commit to tomorrow is...

....

Focus Daily Planner

Date: .... / .... / ....

Affirmation – Today's message to myself:

....

....

....

....

Communication – Who must I communicate with today?

....

....

....

Execution

What tasks must be done today?

....

....

....

What actions do I need to take today to execute on my vision or work strategy?

....

....

....

....

....

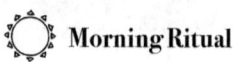 Morning Ritual

One thing I can get excited about today is...

....

I am grateful this morning because...

....

The word that best describes the person I want to be today is...

....

One bold action I can take today is...

....

'Coach me' to myself: Today you need to remember that...

....

I would know today is a good day if...

....

Evening Ritual

Tonight I am grateful because...

....

A situation that I handled well today was...

....

Something I learnt today was...

....

I could have made today even better by...

....

One thing I will let go of for tomorrow is...

....

One thing I will commit to tomorrow is...

....

Focus Daily Planner

Date: .... / .... / ....

Affirmation – Today's message to myself:

....

....

....

....

Communication – Who must I communicate with today?

....

....

....

Execution

What tasks must be done today?

....

....

....

What actions do I need to take today to execute on my vision or work strategy?

....

....

....

....

....

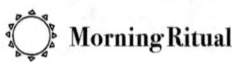 Morning Ritual

One thing I can get excited about today is...

....

I am grateful this morning because...

....

The word that best describes the person I want to be today is...

....

One bold action I can take today is...

....

'Coach me' to myself: Today you need to remember that...

....

I would know today is a good day if...

....

☾ Evening Ritual

Tonight I am grateful because...

....

A situation that I handled well today was...

....

Something I learnt today was...

....

I could have made today even better by...

....

One thing I will let go of for tomorrow is...

....

One thing I will commit to tomorrow is...

....

Focus Daily Planner

Date: .... / .... / ....

Affirmation – Today's message to myself:

....
....
....
....

Communication – Who must I communicate with today?

....
....
....

Execution

What tasks must be done today?

....
....
....

What actions do I need to take today to execute on my vision or work strategy?

....
....
....
....
....

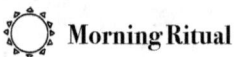 **Morning Ritual**

One thing I can get excited about today is...

....

I am grateful this morning because...

....

The word that best describes the person I want to be today is...

....

One bold action I can take today is...

....

'Coach me' to myself: Today you need to remember that...

....

I would know today is a good day if...

....

Evening Ritual

Tonight I am grateful because...

....

A situation that I handled well today was...

....

Something I learnt today was...

....

I could have made today even better by...

....

One thing I will let go of for tomorrow is...

....

One thing I will commit to tomorrow is...

....

Focus Daily Planner

Date: .... / .... / ....

Affirmation – Today's message to myself:

....
....
....
....

Communication – Who must I communicate with today?

....
....
....

Execution

What tasks must be done today?

....
....
....

What actions do I need to take today to execute on my vision or work strategy?

....
....
....
....
....

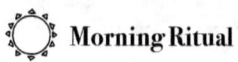 Morning Ritual

One thing I can get excited about today is...

....

I am grateful this morning because...

....

The word that best describes the person I want to be today is...

....

One bold action I can take today is...

....

'Coach me' to myself: Today you need to remember that...

....

I would know today is a good day if...

....

Evening Ritual

Tonight I am grateful because...

....

A situation that I handled well today was...

....

Something I learnt today was...

....

I could have made today even better by...

....

One thing I will let go of for tomorrow is...

....

One thing I will commit to tomorrow is...

....

Focus Daily Planner

Date: .... / .... / ....

Affirmation – Today's message to myself:

....

....

....

....

Communication – Who must I communicate with today?

....

....

....

Execution

What tasks must be done today?

....

....

....

What actions do I need to take today to execute on my vision or work strategy?

....

....

....

....

....

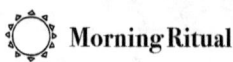
Morning Ritual

One thing I can get excited about today is...

....

I am grateful this morning because...

....

The word that best describes the person I want to be today is...

....

One bold action I can take today is...

....

'Coach me' to myself: Today you need to remember that...

....

I would know today is a good day if...

....

Evening Ritual

Tonight I am grateful because...

....

A situation that I handled well today was...

....

Something I learnt today was...

....

I could have made today even better by...

....

One thing I will let go of for tomorrow is...

....

One thing I will commit to tomorrow is...

....

Focus Daily Planner

Date: ………. / ………. / ……….

Affirmation – Today's message to myself:

....

....

....

....

Communication – Who must I communicate with today?

....

....

....

Execution

What tasks must be done today?

....

....

....

What actions do I need to take today to execute on my vision or work strategy?

....

....

....

....

....

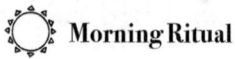 **Morning Ritual**

One thing I can get excited about today is...

....

I am grateful this morning because...

....

The word that best describes the person I want to be today is...

....

One bold action I can take today is...

....

'Coach me' to myself: Today you need to remember that...

....

I would know today is a good day if...

....

Evening Ritual

Tonight I am grateful because...

....

A situation that I handled well today was...

....

Something I learnt today was...

....

I could have made today even better by...

....

One thing I will let go of for tomorrow is...

....

One thing I will commit to tomorrow is...

....

Focus Daily Planner

Date: .... / .... / ....

Affirmation – Today's message to myself:

....

....

....

....

Communication – Who must I communicate with today?

....

....

....

Execution

What tasks must be done today?

....

....

....

What actions do I need to take today to execute on my vision or work strategy?

....

....

....

....

....

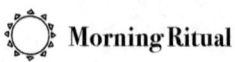 Morning Ritual

One thing I can get excited about today is...

....

I am grateful this morning because...

....

The word that best describes the person I want to be today is...

....

One bold action I can take today is...

....

'Coach me' to myself: Today you need to remember that...

....

I would know today is a good day if...

....

Evening Ritual

Tonight I am grateful because...

....

A situation that I handled well today was...

....

Something I learnt today was...

....

I could have made today even better by...

....

One thing I will let go of for tomorrow is...

....

One thing I will commit to tomorrow is...

....

Focus Daily Planner

Date: .... / .... / ....

Affirmation – Today's message to myself:

....

....

....

....

Communication – Who must I communicate with today?

....

....

....

Execution

What tasks must be done today?

....

....

....

What actions do I need to take today to execute on my vision or work strategy?

....

....

....

....

....

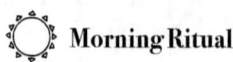

Morning Ritual

One thing I can get excited about today is…

....

I am grateful this morning because…

....

The word that best describes the person I want to be today is…

....

One bold action I can take today is…

....

'Coach me' to myself: Today you need to remember that…

....

I would know today is a good day if…

....

Evening Ritual

Tonight I am grateful because…

....

A situation that I handled well today was…

....

Something I learnt today was…

....

I could have made today even better by…

....

One thing I will let go of for tomorrow is…

....

One thing I will commit to tomorrow is…

....

Focus Daily Planner

Date: .... / .... / ....

Affirmation – Today's message to myself:

....

....

....

....

Communication – Who must I communicate with today?

....

....

....

Execution

What tasks must be done today?

....

....

....

What actions do I need to take today to execute on my vision or work strategy?

....

....

....

....

....

 **Morning Ritual**

One thing I can get excited about today is...

....

I am grateful this morning because...

....

The word that best describes the person I want to be today is...

....

One bold action I can take today is...

....

'Coach me' to myself: Today you need to remember that...

....

I would know today is a good day if...

....

Evening Ritual

Tonight I am grateful because...

....

A situation that I handled well today was...

....

Something I learnt today was...

....

I could have made today even better by...

....

One thing I will let go of for tomorrow is...

....

One thing I will commit to tomorrow is...

....

Focus Daily Planner

Date: .... / .... / ....

Affirmation – Today's message to myself:

....

....

....

....

Communication – Who must I communicate with today?

....

....

....

Execution

What tasks must be done today?

....

....

....

What actions do I need to take today to execute on my vision or work strategy?

....

....

....

....

....

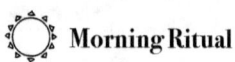 Morning Ritual

One thing I can get excited about today is...

....

I am grateful this morning because...

....

The word that best describes the person I want to be today is...

....

One bold action I can take today is...

....

'Coach me' to myself: Today you need to remember that...

....

I would know today is a good day if...

....

Evening Ritual

Tonight I am grateful because...

....

A situation that I handled well today was...

....

Something I learnt today was...

....

I could have made today even better by...

....

One thing I will let go of for tomorrow is...

....

One thing I will commit to tomorrow is...

....

Focus Daily Planner

Date: .... / .... / ....

Affirmation – Today's message to myself:

....

....

....

....

Communication – Who must I communicate with today?

....

....

....

Execution

What tasks must be done today?

....

....

....

What actions do I need to take today to execute on my vision or work strategy?

....

....

....

....

....

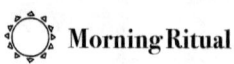 **Morning Ritual**

One thing I can get excited about today is...

....

I am grateful this morning because...

....

The word that best describes the person I want to be today is...

....

One bold action I can take today is...

....

'Coach me' to myself: Today you need to remember that...

....

I would know today is a good day if...

....

☾ Evening Ritual

Tonight I am grateful because...

....

A situation that I handled well today was...

....

Something I learnt today was...

....

I could have made today even better by...

....

One thing I will let go of for tomorrow is...

....

One thing I will commit to tomorrow is...

....

Focus Daily Planner

Date: .... / .... / ....

Affirmation – Today's message to myself:

....
....
....
....

Communication – Who must I communicate with today?

....
....
....

Execution

What tasks must be done today?

....
....
....

What actions do I need to take today to execute on my vision or work strategy?

....
....
....
....
....

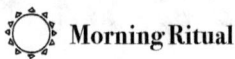 Morning Ritual

One thing I can get excited about today is…

....

I am grateful this morning because…

....

The word that best describes the person I want to be today is…

....

One bold action I can take today is…

....

'Coach me' to myself: Today you need to remember that…

....

I would know today is a good day if…

....

☾ Evening Ritual

Tonight I am grateful because…

....

A situation that I handled well today was…

....

Something I learnt today was…

....

I could have made today even better by…

....

One thing I will let go of for tomorrow is…

....

One thing I will commit to tomorrow is…

....

Focus Daily Planner

Date: .... / .... / ....

Affirmation – Today's message to myself:

....
....
....
....

Communication – Who must I communicate with today?

....
....
....

Execution

What tasks must be done today?

....
....
....

What actions do I need to take today to execute on my vision or work strategy?

....
....
....
....
....

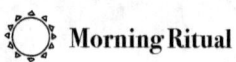 Morning Ritual

One thing I can get excited about today is…

....

I am grateful this morning because…

....

The word that best describes the person I want to be today is…

....

One bold action I can take today is…

....

'Coach me' to myself: Today you need to remember that…

....

I would know today is a good day if…

....

Evening Ritual

Tonight I am grateful because…

....

A situation that I handled well today was…

....

Something I learnt today was…

....

I could have made today even better by…

....

One thing I will let go of for tomorrow is…

....

One thing I will commit to tomorrow is…

....

Focus Daily Planner

Date: .... / .... / ....

Affirmation – Today's message to myself:

....

....

....

....

Communication – Who must I communicate with today?

....

....

....

Execution

What tasks must be done today?

....

....

....

What actions do I need to take today to execute on my vision or work strategy?

....

....

....

....

....

 Morning Ritual

One thing I can get excited about today is...

....

I am grateful this morning because...

....

The word that best describes the person I want to be today is...

....

One bold action I can take today is...

....

'Coach me' to myself: Today you need to remember that...

....

I would know today is a good day if...

....

☾ Evening Ritual

Tonight I am grateful because...

....

A situation that I handled well today was...

....

Something I learnt today was...

....

I could have made today even better by...

....

One thing I will let go of for tomorrow is...

....

One thing I will commit to tomorrow is...

....

Focus Daily Planner

Date: .... / .... / ....

Affirmation – Today's message to myself:

....

....

....

....

Communication – Who must I communicate with today?

....

....

....

Execution

What tasks must be done today?

....

....

....

What actions do I need to take today to execute on my vision or work strategy?

....

....

....

....

....

 **Morning Ritual**

One thing I can get excited about today is...

....

I am grateful this morning because...

....

The word that best describes the person I want to be today is...

....

One bold action I can take today is...

....

'Coach me' to myself: Today you need to remember that...

....

I would know today is a good day if...

....

☾ Evening Ritual

Tonight I am grateful because...

....

A situation that I handled well today was...

....

Something I learnt today was...

....

I could have made today even better by...

....

One thing I will let go of for tomorrow is...

....

One thing I will commit to tomorrow is...

....

Focus Daily Planner

Date: .... / .... / ....

Affirmation – Today's message to myself:

....

....

....

....

Communication – Who must I communicate with today?

....

....

....

Execution

What tasks must be done today?

....

....

....

What actions do I need to take today to execute on my vision or work strategy?

....

....

....

....

....

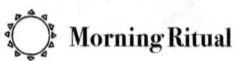 Morning Ritual

One thing I can get excited about today is…

....

I am grateful this morning because…

....

The word that best describes the person I want to be today is…

....

One bold action I can take today is…

....

'Coach me' to myself: Today you need to remember that…

....

I would know today is a good day if…

....

Evening Ritual

Tonight I am grateful because…

....

A situation that I handled well today was…

....

Something I learnt today was…

....

I could have made today even better by…

....

One thing I will let go of for tomorrow is…

....

One thing I will commit to tomorrow is…

....

Focus Daily Planner

Date: .... / .... / ....

Affirmation – Today's message to myself:

....
....
....
....

Communication – Who must I communicate with today?

....
....
....

Execution

What tasks must be done today?

....
....
....

What actions do I need to take today to execute on my vision or work strategy?

....
....
....
....
....

 **Morning Ritual**

One thing I can get excited about today is...

....

I am grateful this morning because...

....

The word that best describes the person I want to be today is...

....

One bold action I can take today is...

....

'Coach me' to myself: Today you need to remember that...

....

I would know today is a good day if...

....

☾ Evening Ritual

Tonight I am grateful because...

....

A situation that I handled well today was...

....

Something I learnt today was...

....

I could have made today even better by...

....

One thing I will let go of for tomorrow is...

....

One thing I will commit to tomorrow is...

....

Focus Daily Planner

Date: .... / .... / ....

Affirmation – Today's message to myself:

....

....

....

....

Communication – Who must I communicate with today?

....

....

....

👁 Execution

What tasks must be done today?

....

....

....

What actions do I need to take today to execute on my vision or work strategy?

....

....

....

....

....

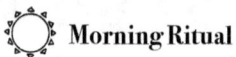 Morning Ritual

One thing I can get excited about today is...

....

I am grateful this morning because...

....

The word that best describes the person I want to be today is...

....

One bold action I can take today is...

....

'Coach me' to myself: Today you need to remember that...

....

I would know today is a good day if...

....

Evening Ritual

Tonight I am grateful because...

....

A situation that I handled well today was...

....

Something I learnt today was...

....

I could have made today even better by...

....

One thing I will let go of for tomorrow is...

....

One thing I will commit to tomorrow is...

....

Focus Daily Planner

Date: .... / .... / ....

Affirmation – Today's message to myself:

....

....

....

....

Communication – Who must I communicate with today?

....

....

....

Execution

What tasks must be done today?

....

....

....

What actions do I need to take today to execute on my vision or work strategy?

....

....

....

....

....

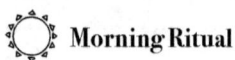
Morning Ritual

One thing I can get excited about today is...

....

I am grateful this morning because...

....

The word that best describes the person I want to be today is...

....

One bold action I can take today is...

....

'Coach me' to myself: Today you need to remember that...

....

I would know today is a good day if...

....

Evening Ritual

Tonight I am grateful because...

....

A situation that I handled well today was...

....

Something I learnt today was...

....

I could have made today even better by...

....

One thing I will let go of for tomorrow is...

....

One thing I will commit to tomorrow is...

....

Focus Daily Planner

Date: .... / .... / ....

Affirmation – Today's message to myself:

....

....

....

....

Communication – Who must I communicate with today?

....

....

....

Execution

What tasks must be done today?

....

....

....

What actions do I need to take today to execute on my vision or work strategy?

....

....

....

....

....

 **Morning Ritual**

One thing I can get excited about today is...

....

I am grateful this morning because...

....

The word that best describes the person I want to be today is...

....

One bold action I can take today is...

....

'Coach me' to myself: Today you need to remember that...

....

I would know today is a good day if...

....

☾ Evening Ritual

Tonight I am grateful because...

....

A situation that I handled well today was...

....

Something I learnt today was...

....

I could have made today even better by...

....

One thing I will let go of for tomorrow is...

....

One thing I will commit to tomorrow is...

....

Focus Daily Planner

Date: .... / .... / ....

Affirmation – Today's message to myself:

....

....

....

....

Communication – Who must I communicate with today?

....

....

....

Execution

What tasks must be done today?

....

....

....

What actions do I need to take today to execute on my vision or work strategy?

....

....

....

....

....

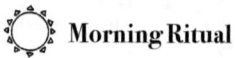 **Morning Ritual**

One thing I can get excited about today is…

....

I am grateful this morning because…

....

The word that best describes the person I want to be today is…

....

One bold action I can take today is…

....

'Coach me' to myself: Today you need to remember that…

....

I would know today is a good day if…

....

☾ Evening Ritual

Tonight I am grateful because…

....

A situation that I handled well today was…

....

Something I learnt today was…

....

I could have made today even better by…

....

One thing I will let go of for tomorrow is…

....

One thing I will commit to tomorrow is…

....

Focus Daily Planner

Date: .... / .... / ....

Affirmation – Today's message to myself:

....

....

....

....

Communication – Who must I communicate with today?

....

....

....

Execution

What tasks must be done today?

....

....

....

What actions do I need to take today to execute on my vision or work strategy?

....

....

....

....

....

 Morning Ritual

One thing I can get excited about today is...

....

I am grateful this morning because...

....

The word that best describes the person I want to be today is...

....

One bold action I can take today is...

....

'Coach me' to myself: Today you need to remember that...

....

I would know today is a good day if...

....

☾ Evening Ritual

Tonight I am grateful because...

....

A situation that I handled well today was...

....

Something I learnt today was...

....

I could have made today even better by...

....

One thing I will let go of for tomorrow is...

....

One thing I will commit to tomorrow is...

....

Focus Daily Planner

Date: ………… / ………… / …………

Affirmation – Today's message to myself:

....

....

....

....

Communication – Who must I communicate with today?

....

....

....

👁 Execution

What tasks must be done today?

....

....

....

What actions do I need to take today to execute on my vision or work strategy?

....

....

....

....

....

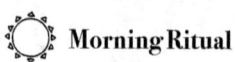 Morning Ritual

One thing I can get excited about today is...

....

I am grateful this morning because...

....

The word that best describes the person I want to be today is...

....

One bold action I can take today is...

....

'Coach me' to myself: Today you need to remember that...

....

I would know today is a good day if...

....

☾ Evening Ritual

Tonight I am grateful because...

....

A situation that I handled well today was...

....

Something I learnt today was...

....

I could have made today even better by...

....

One thing I will let go of for tomorrow is...

....

One thing I will commit to tomorrow is...

....

Focus Daily Planner

Date: .... / .... / ....

Affirmation – Today's message to myself:

....
....
....
....

Communication – Who must I communicate with today?

....
....
....

Execution

What tasks must be done today?

....
....
....

What actions do I need to take today to execute on my vision or work strategy?

....
....
....
....
....

Morning Ritual

One thing I can get excited about today is...

....

I am grateful this morning because...

....

The word that best describes the person I want to be today is...

....

One bold action I can take today is...

....

'Coach me' to myself: Today you need to remember that...

....

I would know today is a good day if...

....

Evening Ritual

Tonight I am grateful because...

....

A situation that I handled well today was...

....

Something I learnt today was...

....

I could have made today even better by...

....

One thing I will let go of for tomorrow is...

....

One thing I will commit to tomorrow is...

....

Focus Daily Planner

Date: .... / .... / ....

Affirmation – Today's message to myself:

....

....

....

....

Communication – Who must I communicate with today?

....

....

....

Execution

What tasks must be done today?

....

....

....

What actions do I need to take today to execute on my vision or work strategy?

....

....

....

....

....

☼ Morning Ritual

One thing I can get excited about today is...

....

I am grateful this morning because...

....

The word that best describes the person I want to be today is...

....

One bold action I can take today is...

....

'Coach me' to myself: Today you need to remember that...

....

I would know today is a good day if...

....

☾ Evening Ritual

Tonight I am grateful because...

....

A situation that I handled well today was...

....

Something I learnt today was...

....

I could have made today even better by...

....

One thing I will let go of for tomorrow is...

....

One thing I will commit to tomorrow is...

....

Focus Daily Planner

Date: .... / .... / ....

Affirmation – Today's message to myself:

....

....

....

....

Communication – Who must I communicate with today?

....

....

....

Execution

What tasks must be done today?

....

....

....

What actions do I need to take today to execute on my vision or work strategy?

....

....

....

....

....

Morning Ritual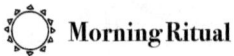

One thing I can get excited about today is...

....

I am grateful this morning because...

....

The word that best describes the person I want to be today is...

....

One bold action I can take today is...

....

'Coach me' to myself: Today you need to remember that...

....

I would know today is a good day if...

....

Evening Ritual

Tonight I am grateful because...

....

A situation that I handled well today was...

....

Something I learnt today was...

....

I could have made today even better by...

....

One thing I will let go of for tomorrow is...

....

One thing I will commit to tomorrow is...

....

Focus Daily Planner

Date: .... / .... / ....

Affirmation – Today's message to myself:

....

....

....

....

Communication – Who must I communicate with today?

....

....

....

👁 Execution

What tasks must be done today?

....

....

....

What actions do I need to take today to execute on my vision or work strategy?

....

....

....

....

 Morning Ritual

One thing I can get excited about today is...

....

I am grateful this morning because...

....

The word that best describes the person I want to be today is...

....

One bold action I can take today is...

....

'Coach me' to myself: Today you need to remember that...

....

I would know today is a good day if...

....

Evening Ritual

Tonight I am grateful because...

....

A situation that I handled well today was...

....

Something I learnt today was...

....

I could have made today even better by...

....

One thing I will let go of for tomorrow is...

....

One thing I will commit to tomorrow is...

....

Focus Daily Planner

Date: .... / .... / ....

Affirmation – Today's message to myself:

....

....

....

....

Communication – Who must I communicate with today?

....

....

....

Execution

What tasks must be done today?

....

....

....

What actions do I need to take today to execute on my vision or work strategy?

....

....

....

....

....

 ## Morning Ritual

One thing I can get excited about today is...

....

I am grateful this morning because...

....

The word that best describes the person I want to be today is...

....

One bold action I can take today is...

....

'Coach me' to myself: Today you need to remember that...

....

I would know today is a good day if...

....

Evening Ritual

Tonight I am grateful because...

....

A situation that I handled well today was...

....

Something I learnt today was...

....

I could have made today even better by...

....

One thing I will let go of for tomorrow is...

....

One thing I will commit to tomorrow is...

....

Focus Daily Planner

Date: .... / .... / ....

Affirmation – Today's message to myself:

....
....
....
....

Communication – Who must I communicate with today?

....
....
....

Execution

What tasks must be done today?

....
....
....

What actions do I need to take today to execute on my vision or work strategy?

....
....
....
....
....

 Morning Ritual

One thing I can get excited about today is...

....

I am grateful this morning because...

....

The word that best describes the person I want to be today is...

....

One bold action I can take today is...

....

'Coach me' to myself: Today you need to remember that...

....

I would know today is a good day if...

....

Evening Ritual

Tonight I am grateful because...

....

A situation that I handled well today was...

....

Something I learnt today was...

....

I could have made today even better by...

....

One thing I will let go of for tomorrow is...

....

One thing I will commit to tomorrow is...

....

Focus Daily Planner

Date: .... / .... / ....

Affirmation – Today's message to myself:

....

....

....

....

Communication – Who must I communicate with today?

....

....

....

Execution

What tasks must be done today?

....

....

....

What actions do I need to take today to execute on my vision or work strategy?

....

....

....

....

....

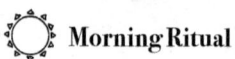 Morning Ritual

One thing I can get excited about today is...

....

I am grateful this morning because...

....

The word that best describes the person I want to be today is...

....

One bold action I can take today is...

....

'Coach me' to myself: Today you need to remember that...

....

I would know today is a good day if...

....

Evening Ritual

Tonight I am grateful because...

....

A situation that I handled well today was...

....

Something I learnt today was...

....

I could have made today even better by...

....

One thing I will let go of for tomorrow is...

....

One thing I will commit to tomorrow is...

....

Focus Daily Planner

Date: .... / .... / ....

Affirmation – Today's message to myself:

....
....
....
....

Communication – Who must I communicate with today?

....
....
....

Execution

What tasks must be done today?

....
....
....

What actions do I need to take today to execute on my vision or work strategy?

....
....
....
....
....

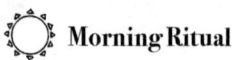 Morning Ritual

One thing I can get excited about today is...

....

I am grateful this morning because...

....

The word that best describes the person I want to be today is...

....

One bold action I can take today is...

....

'Coach me' to myself: Today you need to remember that...

....

I would know today is a good day if...

....

Evening Ritual

Tonight I am grateful because...

....

A situation that I handled well today was...

....

Something I learnt today was...

....

I could have made today even better by...

....

One thing I will let go of for tomorrow is...

....

One thing I will commit to tomorrow is...

....

Focus Daily Planner

Date: .... / .... / ....

Affirmation – Today's message to myself:

....

....

....

....

Communication – Who must I communicate with today?

....

....

....

Execution

What tasks must be done today?

....

....

....

What actions do I need to take today to execute on my vision or work strategy?

....

....

....

....

....

 **Morning Ritual**

One thing I can get excited about today is...

....

I am grateful this morning because...

....

The word that best describes the person I want to be today is...

....

One bold action I can take today is...

....

'Coach me' to myself: Today you need to remember that...

....

I would know today is a good day if...

....

☾ Evening Ritual

Tonight I am grateful because...

....

A situation that I handled well today was...

....

Something I learnt today was...

....

I could have made today even better by...

....

One thing I will let go of for tomorrow is...

....

One thing I will commit to tomorrow is...

....

Focus Daily Planner

Date: ………… / ………… / …………

Affirmation – Today's message to myself:

……………………………………………………………………………………………………
……………………………………………………………………………………………………
……………………………………………………………………………………………………
……………………………………………………………………………………………………

Communication – Who must I communicate with today?

……………………………………………………………………………………………………
……………………………………………………………………………………………………
……………………………………………………………………………………………………

Execution

What tasks must be done today?

……………………………………………………………………………………………………
……………………………………………………………………………………………………
……………………………………………………………………………………………………

What actions do I need to take today to execute on my vision or work strategy?

……………………………………………………………………………………………………
……………………………………………………………………………………………………
……………………………………………………………………………………………………
……………………………………………………………………………………………………
……………………………………………………………………………………………………

 Morning Ritual

One thing I can get excited about today is...

....

I am grateful this morning because...

....

The word that best describes the person I want to be today is...

....

One bold action I can take today is...

....

'Coach me' to myself: Today you need to remember that...

....

I would know today is a good day if...

....

Evening Ritual

Tonight I am grateful because...

....

A situation that I handled well today was...

....

Something I learnt today was...

....

I could have made today even better by...

....

One thing I will let go of for tomorrow is...

....

One thing I will commit to tomorrow is...

....

›! **Focus Daily Planner**

Date: .... / .... / ....

Affirmation – Today's message to myself:

....

....

....

....

Communication – Who must I communicate with today?

....

....

....

👁 Execution

What tasks must be done today?

....

....

....

What actions do I need to take today to execute on my vision or work strategy?

....

....

....

....

....

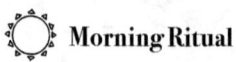 Morning Ritual

One thing I can get excited about today is…
....

I am grateful this morning because…
....

The word that best describes the person I want to be today is…
....

One bold action I can take today is…
....

'Coach me' to myself: Today you need to remember that…
....

I would know today is a good day if…
....

☾ Evening Ritual

Tonight I am grateful because…
....

A situation that I handled well today was…
....

Something I learnt today was…
....

I could have made today even better by…
....

One thing I will let go of for tomorrow is…
....

One thing I will commit to tomorrow is…
....

Focus Daily Planner

Date: .... / .... / ....

Affirmation – Today's message to myself:

....

....

....

....

Communication – Who must I communicate with today?

....

....

....

Execution

What tasks must be done today?

....

....

....

What actions do I need to take today to execute on my vision or work strategy?

....

....

....

....

....

Morning Ritual

One thing I can get excited about today is...

....

I am grateful this morning because...

....

The word that best describes the person I want to be today is...

....

One bold action I can take today is...

....

'Coach me' to myself: Today you need to remember that...

....

I would know today is a good day if...

....

Evening Ritual

Tonight I am grateful because...

....

A situation that I handled well today was...

....

Something I learnt today was...

....

I could have made today even better by...

....

One thing I will let go of for tomorrow is...

....

One thing I will commit to tomorrow is...

....

Focus Daily Planner

Date: .... / .... / ....

Affirmation – Today's message to myself:

....
....
....
....

Communication – Who must I communicate with today?

....
....
....

Execution

What tasks must be done today?

....
....
....

What actions do I need to take today to execute on my vision or work strategy?

....
....
....
....
....

 Morning Ritual

One thing I can get excited about today is…

....

I am grateful this morning because…

....

The word that best describes the person I want to be today is…

....

One bold action I can take today is…

....

'Coach me' to myself: Today you need to remember that…

....

I would know today is a good day if…

....

☾ Evening Ritual

Tonight I am grateful because…

....

A situation that I handled well today was…

....

Something I learnt today was…

....

I could have made today even better by…

....

One thing I will let go of for tomorrow is…

....

One thing I will commit to tomorrow is…

....

Focus Daily Planner

Date: .... / .... / ....

Affirmation – Today's message to myself:

....

....

....

....

Communication – Who must I communicate with today?

....

....

....

Execution

What tasks must be done today?

....

....

....

What actions do I need to take today to execute on my vision or work strategy?

....

....

....

....

....

 Morning Ritual

One thing I can get excited about today is...

....

I am grateful this morning because...

....

The word that best describes the person I want to be today is...

....

One bold action I can take today is...

....

'Coach me' to myself: Today you need to remember that...

....

I would know today is a good day if...

....

☾ Evening Ritual

Tonight I am grateful because...

....

A situation that I handled well today was...

....

Something I learnt today was...

....

I could have made today even better by...

....

One thing I will let go of for tomorrow is...

....

One thing I will commit to tomorrow is...

....

Focus Daily Planner

Date: .... / .... / ....

Affirmation – Today's message to myself:

....

....

....

....

Communication – Who must I communicate with today?

....

....

....

Execution

What tasks must be done today?

....

....

....

What actions do I need to take today to execute on my vision or work strategy?

....

....

....

....

....

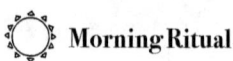 **Morning Ritual**

One thing I can get excited about today is...
....

I am grateful this morning because...
....

The word that best describes the person I want to be today is...
....

One bold action I can take today is...
....

'Coach me' to myself: Today you need to remember that...
....

I would know today is a good day if...
....

☾ Evening Ritual

Tonight I am grateful because...
....

A situation that I handled well today was...
....

Something I learnt today was...
....

I could have made today even better by...
....

One thing I will let go of for tomorrow is...
....

One thing I will commit to tomorrow is...
....

Focus Daily Planner

Date: .... / .... / ....

Affirmation – Today's message to myself:

....
....
....
....

Communication – Who must I communicate with today?

....
....
....

Execution

What tasks must be done today?

....
....
....

What actions do I need to take today to execute on my vision or work strategy?

....
....
....
....
....

 Morning Ritual

One thing I can get excited about today is...

....

I am grateful this morning because...

....

The word that best describes the person I want to be today is...

....

One bold action I can take today is...

....

'Coach me' to myself: Today you need to remember that...

....

I would know today is a good day if...

....

Evening Ritual

Tonight I am grateful because...

....

A situation that I handled well today was...

....

Something I learnt today was...

....

I could have made today even better by...

....

One thing I will let go of for tomorrow is...

....

One thing I will commit to tomorrow is...

....

Focus Daily Planner

Date: .... / .... / ....

Affirmation – Today's message to myself:

....

....

....

....

Communication – Who must I communicate with today?

....

....

....

Execution

What tasks must be done today?

....

....

....

What actions do I need to take today to execute on my vision or work strategy?

....

....

....

....

....

 **Morning Ritual**

One thing I can get excited about today is...

....

I am grateful this morning because...

....

The word that best describes the person I want to be today is...

....

One bold action I can take today is...

....

'Coach me' to myself: Today you need to remember that...

....

I would know today is a good day if...

....

☾ Evening Ritual

Tonight I am grateful because...

....

A situation that I handled well today was...

....

Something I learnt today was...

....

I could have made today even better by...

....

One thing I will let go of for tomorrow is...

....

One thing I will commit to tomorrow is...

....

Focus Daily Planner

Date: .... / .... / ....

Affirmation – Today's message to myself:

....
....
....
....

Communication – Who must I communicate with today?

....
....
....

Execution

What tasks must be done today?

....
....
....

What actions do I need to take today to execute on my vision or work strategy?

....
....
....
....
....

Morning Ritual

One thing I can get excited about today is...

....

I am grateful this morning because...

....

The word that best describes the person I want to be today is...

....

One bold action I can take today is...

....

'Coach me' to myself: Today you need to remember that...

....

I would know today is a good day if...

....

Evening Ritual

Tonight I am grateful because...

....

A situation that I handled well today was...

....

Something I learnt today was...

....

I could have made today even better by...

....

One thing I will let go of for tomorrow is...

....

One thing I will commit to tomorrow is...

....

Focus Daily Planner

Date: .... / .... / ....

Affirmation – Today's message to myself:

....

....

....

....

Communication – Who must I communicate with today?

....

....

....

Execution

What tasks must be done today?

....

....

....

What actions do I need to take today to execute on my vision or work strategy?

....

....

....

....

....

 Morning Ritual

One thing I can get excited about today is...

....

I am grateful this morning because...

....

The word that best describes the person I want to be today is...

....

One bold action I can take today is...

....

'Coach me' to myself: Today you need to remember that...

....

I would know today is a good day if...

....

☾ Evening Ritual

Tonight I am grateful because...

....

A situation that I handled well today was...

....

Something I learnt today was...

....

I could have made today even better by...

....

One thing I will let go of for tomorrow is...

....

One thing I will commit to tomorrow is...

....

Focus Daily Planner

Date: .... / .... / ....

Affirmation – Today's message to myself:

....
....
....
....

Communication – Who must I communicate with today?

....
....
....

Execution

What tasks must be done today?

....
....
....

What actions do I need to take today to execute on my vision or work strategy?

....
....
....
....
....

Morning Ritual

One thing I can get excited about today is...

....

I am grateful this morning because...

....

The word that best describes the person I want to be today is...

....

One bold action I can take today is...

....

'Coach me' to myself: Today you need to remember that...

....

I would know today is a good day if...

....

Evening Ritual

Tonight I am grateful because...

....

A situation that I handled well today was...

....

Something I learnt today was...

....

I could have made today even better by...

....

One thing I will let go of for tomorrow is...

....

One thing I will commit to tomorrow is...

....

Focus Daily Planner

Date: .... / .... / ....

Affirmation – Today's message to myself:

....

....

....

....

Communication – Who must I communicate with today?

....

....

....

Execution

What tasks must be done today?

....

....

....

What actions do I need to take today to execute on my vision or work strategy?

....

....

....

....

....

 Morning Ritual

One thing I can get excited about today is…

....

I am grateful this morning because…

....

The word that best describes the person I want to be today is…

....

One bold action I can take today is…

....

'Coach me' to myself: Today you need to remember that…

....

I would know today is a good day if…

....

Evening Ritual

Tonight I am grateful because…

....

A situation that I handled well today was…

....

Something I learnt today was…

....

I could have made today even better by…

....

One thing I will let go of for tomorrow is…

....

One thing I will commit to tomorrow is…

....

Focus Daily Planner

Date: .... / .... / ....

Affirmation – Today's message to myself:

....

....

....

....

Communication – Who must I communicate with today?

....

....

....

Execution

What tasks must be done today?

....

....

....

What actions do I need to take today to execute on my vision or work strategy?

....

....

....

....

....

 Morning Ritual

One thing I can get excited about today is...

....

I am grateful this morning because...

....

The word that best describes the person I want to be today is...

....

One bold action I can take today is...

....

'Coach me' to myself: Today you need to remember that...

....

I would know today is a good day if...

....

☾ Evening Ritual

Tonight I am grateful because...

....

A situation that I handled well today was...

....

Something I learnt today was...

....

I could have made today even better by...

....

One thing I will let go of for tomorrow is...

....

One thing I will commit to tomorrow is...

....

Focus Daily Planner

Date: .... / .... / ....

Affirmation – Today's message to myself:

....

....

....

....

Communication – Who must I communicate with today?

....

....

....

Execution

What tasks must be done today?

....

....

....

What actions do I need to take today to execute on my vision or work strategy?

....

....

....

....

....

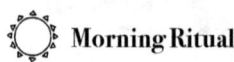 **Morning Ritual**

One thing I can get excited about today is…

....

I am grateful this morning because…

....

The word that best describes the person I want to be today is…

....

One bold action I can take today is…

....

'Coach me' to myself: Today you need to remember that…

....

I would know today is a good day if…

....

☾ Evening Ritual

Tonight I am grateful because…

....

A situation that I handled well today was…

....

Something I learnt today was…

....

I could have made today even better by…

....

One thing I will let go of for tomorrow is…

....

One thing I will commit to tomorrow is…

....

Focus Daily Planner

Date: ………… / ………… / …………

Affirmation – Today's message to myself:

....

....

....

....

Communication – Who must I communicate with today?

....

....

....

Execution

What tasks must be done today?

....

....

....

What actions do I need to take today to execute on my vision or work strategy?

....

....

....

....

....

 **Morning Ritual**

One thing I can get excited about today is…

....

I am grateful this morning because…

....

The word that best describes the person I want to be today is…

....

One bold action I can take today is…

....

'Coach me' to myself: Today you need to remember that…

....

I would know today is a good day if…

....

☾ Evening Ritual

Tonight I am grateful because…

....

A situation that I handled well today was…

....

Something I learnt today was…

....

I could have made today even better by…

....

One thing I will let go of for tomorrow is…

....

One thing I will commit to tomorrow is…

....

Focus Daily Planner

Date: .... / .... / ....

Affirmation – Today's message to myself:

....
....
....
....

Communication – Who must I communicate with today?

....
....
....

Execution

What tasks must be done today?

....
....
....

What actions do I need to take today to execute on my vision or work strategy?

....
....
....
....
....

 Morning Ritual

One thing I can get excited about today is...

....

I am grateful this morning because...

....

The word that best describes the person I want to be today is...

....

One bold action I can take today is...

....

'Coach me' to myself: Today you need to remember that...

....

I would know today is a good day if...

....

Evening Ritual

Tonight I am grateful because...

....

A situation that I handled well today was...

....

Something I learnt today was...

....

I could have made today even better by...

....

One thing I will let go of for tomorrow is...

....

One thing I will commit to tomorrow is...

....

Focus Daily Planner

Date: .... / .... / ....

Affirmation – Today's message to myself:

....

....

....

....

Communication – Who must I communicate with today?

....

....

....

Execution

What tasks must be done today?

....

....

....

What actions do I need to take today to execute on my vision or work strategy?

....

....

....

....

....

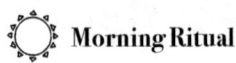 Morning Ritual

One thing I can get excited about today is…

....

I am grateful this morning because…

....

The word that best describes the person I want to be today is…

....

One bold action I can take today is…

....

'Coach me' to myself: Today you need to remember that…

....

I would know today is a good day if…

....

Evening Ritual

Tonight I am grateful because…

....

A situation that I handled well today was…

....

Something I learnt today was…

....

I could have made today even better by…

....

One thing I will let go of for tomorrow is…

....

One thing I will commit to tomorrow is…

....

Focus Daily Planner

Date: .... / .... / ....

Affirmation – Today's message to myself:

....

....

....

....

Communication – Who must I communicate with today?

....

....

....

Execution

What tasks must be done today?

....

....

....

What actions do I need to take today to execute on my vision or work strategy?

....

....

....

....

....

 **Morning Ritual**

One thing I can get excited about today is...

....

I am grateful this morning because...

....

The word that best describes the person I want to be today is...

....

One bold action I can take today is...

....

'Coach me' to myself: Today you need to remember that...

....

I would know today is a good day if...

....

☾ Evening Ritual

Tonight I am grateful because...

....

A situation that I handled well today was...

....

Something I learnt today was...

....

I could have made today even better by...

....

One thing I will let go of for tomorrow is...

....

One thing I will commit to tomorrow is...

....

Focus Daily Planner

Date: .... / .... / ....

Affirmation – Today's message to myself:

....

....

....

....

Communication – Who must I communicate with today?

....

....

....

Execution

What tasks must be done today?

....

....

....

What actions do I need to take today to execute on my vision or work strategy?

....

....

....

....

....

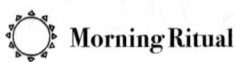

Morning Ritual

One thing I can get excited about today is…

··

I am grateful this morning because…

··

The word that best describes the person I want to be today is…

··

One bold action I can take today is…

··

'Coach me' to myself: Today you need to remember that…

··

I would know today is a good day if…

··

Evening Ritual

Tonight I am grateful because…

··

A situation that I handled well today was…

··

Something I learnt today was…

··

I could have made today even better by…

··

One thing I will let go of for tomorrow is…

··

One thing I will commit to tomorrow is…

··

Focus Daily Planner

Date: .... / .... / ....

Affirmation – Today's message to myself:

....
....
....
....

Communication – Who must I communicate with today?

....
....
....

Execution

What tasks must be done today?

....
....
....

What actions do I need to take today to execute on my vision or work strategy?

....
....
....
....
....

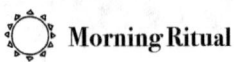 Morning Ritual

One thing I can get excited about today is...

....

I am grateful this morning because...

....

The word that best describes the person I want to be today is...

....

One bold action I can take today is...

....

'Coach me' to myself: Today you need to remember that...

....

I would know today is a good day if...

....

☾ Evening Ritual

Tonight I am grateful because...

....

A situation that I handled well today was...

....

Something I learnt today was...

....

I could have made today even better by...

....

One thing I will let go of for tomorrow is...

....

One thing I will commit to tomorrow is...

....

Focus Daily Planner

Date: .... / .... / ....

Affirmation – Today's message to myself:

....

....

....

....

Communication – Who must I communicate with today?

....

....

....

Execution

What tasks must be done today?

....

....

....

What actions do I need to take today to execute on my vision or work strategy?

....

....

....

....

....

 Morning Ritual

One thing I can get excited about today is…

....

I am grateful this morning because…

....

The word that best describes the person I want to be today is…

....

One bold action I can take today is…

....

'Coach me' to myself: Today you need to remember that…

....

I would know today is a good day if…

....

Evening Ritual

Tonight I am grateful because…

....

A situation that I handled well today was…

....

Something I learnt today was…

....

I could have made today even better by…

....

One thing I will let go of for tomorrow is…

....

One thing I will commit to tomorrow is…

....

Focus Daily Planner

Date: .... / .... / ....

Affirmation – Today's message to myself:

....

....

....

....

Communication – Who must I communicate with today?

....

....

....

Execution

What tasks must be done today?

....

....

....

What actions do I need to take today to execute on my vision or work strategy?

....

....

....

....

....

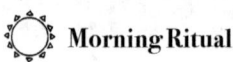 Morning Ritual

One thing I can get excited about today is...

....

I am grateful this morning because...

....

The word that best describes the person I want to be today is...

....

One bold action I can take today is...

....

'Coach me' to myself: Today you need to remember that...

....

I would know today is a good day if...

....

Evening Ritual

Tonight I am grateful because...

....

A situation that I handled well today was...

....

Something I learnt today was...

....

I could have made today even better by...

....

One thing I will let go of for tomorrow is...

....

One thing I will commit to tomorrow is...

....

Focus Daily Planner

Date: .... / .... / ....

Affirmation – Today's message to myself:

....

....

....

....

Communication – Who must I communicate with today?

....

....

....

Execution

What tasks must be done today?

....

....

....

What actions do I need to take today to execute on my vision or work strategy?

....

....

....

....

....

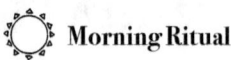 Morning Ritual

One thing I can get excited about today is...

....

I am grateful this morning because...

....

The word that best describes the person I want to be today is...

....

One bold action I can take today is...

....

'Coach me' to myself: Today you need to remember that...

....

I would know today is a good day if...

....

☾ Evening Ritual

Tonight I am grateful because...

....

A situation that I handled well today was...

....

Something I learnt today was...

....

I could have made today even better by...

....

One thing I will let go of for tomorrow is...

....

One thing I will commit to tomorrow is...

....

Focus Daily Planner

Date: .... / .... / ....

Affirmation – Today's message to myself:

....

....

....

....

Communication – Who must I communicate with today?

....

....

....

Execution

What tasks must be done today?

....

....

....

What actions do I need to take today to execute on my vision or work strategy?

....

....

....

....

....

 Morning Ritual

One thing I can get excited about today is...

....

I am grateful this morning because...

....

The word that best describes the person I want to be today is...

....

One bold action I can take today is...

....

'Coach me' to myself: Today you need to remember that...

....

I would know today is a good day if...

....

Evening Ritual

Tonight I am grateful because...

....

A situation that I handled well today was...

....

Something I learnt today was...

....

I could have made today even better by...

....

One thing I will let go of for tomorrow is...

....

One thing I will commit to tomorrow is...

....

Focus Daily Planner

Date: .... / .... / ....

Affirmation – Today's message to myself:

....

....

....

....

Communication – Who must I communicate with today?

....

....

....

Execution

What tasks must be done today?

....

....

....

What actions do I need to take today to execute on my vision or work strategy?

....

....

....

....

....

 Morning Ritual

One thing I can get excited about today is…

....

I am grateful this morning because…

....

The word that best describes the person I want to be today is…

....

One bold action I can take today is…

....

'Coach me' to myself: Today you need to remember that…

....

I would know today is a good day if…

....

Evening Ritual

Tonight I am grateful because…

....

A situation that I handled well today was…

....

Something I learnt today was…

....

I could have made today even better by…

....

One thing I will let go of for tomorrow is…

....

One thing I will commit to tomorrow is…

....

Focus Daily Planner

Date: .... / .... / ....

Affirmation – Today's message to myself:

....

....

....

....

Communication – Who must I communicate with today?

....

....

....

👁 Execution

What tasks must be done today?

....

....

....

What actions do I need to take today to execute on my vision or work strategy?

....

....

....

....

....

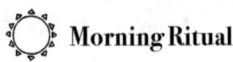 Morning Ritual

One thing I can get excited about today is...

....

I am grateful this morning because...

....

The word that best describes the person I want to be today is...

....

One bold action I can take today is...

....

'Coach me' to myself: Today you need to remember that...

....

I would know today is a good day if...

....

Evening Ritual

Tonight I am grateful because...

....

A situation that I handled well today was...

....

Something I learnt today was...

....

I could have made today even better by...

....

One thing I will let go of for tomorrow is...

....

One thing I will commit to tomorrow is...

....

Focus Daily Planner

Date: .... / .... / ....

Affirmation – Today's message to myself:

....
....
....
....

Communication – Who must I communicate with today?

....
....
....

Execution

What tasks must be done today?

....
....
....

What actions do I need to take today to execute on my vision or work strategy?

....
....
....
....
....

Exercise: The Half Reflection

Take some time to reflect on the last six months. Use your journal entries to notice emerging themes that may suggest areas for future focus. Complete the sections below to build a picture of your common thoughts over the last six months and provide a pathway for the next six months.

Review your responses to the prompt "The word that best describes the person I want to be today is...". Notice any recurring words. Is there a theme that your unconscious mind is presenting to you? This could be an area in which to prioritise mastery.

....

....

....

....

Review your response to "One bold action I can take today is...". Is there a particular area where you are needing to elevate your boldness? Is it with your family? Your team at work? Is it about being more courageous with difficult conversations? The answers here can lead you to an area of self mastery development.

....

....

....

....

'Coach Me' to myself is your internal messaging system from your unconscious mind. What is the recurring message? Is there a series of themes? Pay attention to any clusters that are presenting here.

....

....

....

Reflecting on your evening ritual journaling, what have been the consistent themes in your learning day to day? Are they learnings about yourself, or others? What have been your big highlights?

....

....

....

With every evening ritual, you asked yourself how you could have made your day even better. This is of great importance. If you are seeing recurrences here, this is where you need to shine the light and invest in self mastering.

....

....

....

About Stone Heart, Light Heart

Stone Heart, Light Heart is a guide to awakening and bringing forth your inner power. It brings together the ancient laws of the universe and unites mysticism with psychology. This book will show you how to:

— Find the 'I' within
— Master your mind
— Develop grit and mental toughness
— Succeed by developing your courage to fail
— Defeat fear and self-doubt
— Find your inner warrior
— Forgive and love all that is
— Master the laws of the universe
— Find your purpose
— Develop an unwavering passion to chase your dreams

Stone Heart, Light Heart encompasses the wisdom and truth of the soul. Being true to ourselves and utilising the laws of nature in our daily life will enable us to fulfil our deepest desires.

Stone Heart, Light Heart awakens and strengthens the spiritual dimension within you. Stone Heart is tough and detached; a warrior of spirit, wielding the ability to overcome fear and self-doubt. Stone Heart refuses judgment from others and rejects our self-imposed limitations. Stone Heart is strength.

Light Heart is the spiritual aspect of you that brings forth joy, love and acceptance. Only through the mastery of the mind can one awaken the calm tranquility that Light Heart gifts. Light Heart is love.

When you master both Stone Heart and Light Heart, a power rises within you. *Stone Heart, Light Heart* sheds light on your purpose in life and gives you the unwavering passion to manifest your dreams.

Buy the book at:
stellapetrouconcha.com.au/shop

About the Author

> " The journey of self mastery is taking information and turning it into knowledge, taking knowledge and turning it into wisdom, and taking wisdom and turning it into intelligence. "

stellapetrouconcha.com.au

I have dedicated over twenty years to helping people realise their potential. I work with top executives from some of the world's best-known brands, connecting them to the right people to drive their business forward. Through this work I have gained invaluable insights into what it takes to bring forth your inner power, to find your purpose and to shake off your self-imposed limitations in order to find success. Many of the findings I have implemented in my own career, I have shared with my teams and with the clients and candidates I work with. Now I want to share them with you.

One of the biggest themes of my professional life has been mastering myself by building a positive relationship with failure and detaching from the opinions of others. My success in the corporate world has been facilitated by taking risks and putting myself out there, and alongside that success has come failure, which has delivered more personal and professional growth than I ever could have imagined.

My vision now is to challenge people to embark on their own journey of self mastery. This journey isn't easy. The buck stops with you. I know that only through mastering yourself can you truly thrive and awaken your power.

www.ingramcontent.com/pod-product-compliance
Lightning Source LLC
Chambersburg PA
CBHW071727080526
44588CB00013B/1921